1 MONTH OF
FREE
READING

at
www.ForgottenBooks.com

By purchasing this book you are eligible for one month membership to ForgottenBooks.com, giving you unlimited access to our entire collection of over 1,000,000 titles via our web site and mobile apps.

To claim your free month visit:

www.forgottenbooks.com/free781747

ISBN 978-0-428-78856-8
PIBN 10781747

This book is a reproduction of an important historical work. Forgotten Books uses
state-of-the-art technology to digitally reconstruct the work, preserving the original format
whilst repairing imperfections present in the aged copy. In rare cases, an imperfection in
the original, such as a blemish or missing page, may be replicated in our edition. We do,
however, repair the vast majority of imperfections successfully; any imperfections that
remain are intentionally left to preserve the state of such historical works.

MODEL
BANQUET SPEECHES.

BY

Famous Banquet Speakers.

Thomas A Hendricks & othe

DETROIT:
THE SPRAGUE PUBLISHING COMPANY.
1901.

CONTENTS.

"OUR COUNTRY."

Response by Hon. Thomas A. Hendricks, at a banquet of the Iroquois Club at Chicago, March 15, 1882.

Mr. Chairman and Gentlemen:

You will. no doubt, regard it as appropriate in responding to this toast, to refer to some of the circumstances that especially contribute to our country's greatness and power. Some of the important influences and agencies must, however, be omitted. I cannot so much as make mention of all. The railroads, the telegraphs and the telephones have been heretofore sufficiently discussed.

But, with your permission and approval, we will take a journey upon some of the great lines of railroads. Shall it be from Boston to San Francisco? Seven days and seven nights will pass, as the train flies onward, before we hear the ceaseless murmur of the Pacific. Such a journey, from Paris eastward, would carry us beyond Europe and far into Asia. The line of our travel marks and measures the great extent of our country. The same flag remains over us.

We start from the landing place of the Mayflower, and will stop alongside the great steamers that are in our trade with China and Japan. All the way our hearts are cheered with the music of active industry, and towns and cities are our mile-posts. As we pass New York and Chicago, we take off our hats in recognition of the indomitable genius of daring and successful enterprise. All the way, and in every employment and pursuit, health, energy and courage compel success, and the numerous trains we meet, carrying our products to their markets, answer the inquiry why the balance of trade with foreign countries has been so largely in our favor. On the summit of the mountains, as we gaze upon the distant plains, toward the Atlantic and toward

the Pacific, the spirit of our country is upon us and as-
sures us that in every element of wealth and greatness
we are to lead all the nations, if we but dwell together in
peace and harmony.

San Francisco is the New York of the Pacific Coast.
It commands the commerce of the East and the trade of
the Pacific Slope in its gold and silver products of the
soil. We will go out upon the bay and as far as the Gold-
en Gates. This is the great entrance to our country from
the Pacific. It can be securely defended, and the defenses
already completed are probably impregnable.

We cannot remain longer at San Francisco. Of course
we will return by the Southern route. The next time it
will be by the Northern route. The train cannot wait for
us to visit the vineyards and the orange groves of Los
Angeles, or San Gabriel, or San Bernardino. Fruit of the
richest quality, and wines of choice flavor and of great
value are here produced. I cannot conceive of anything,
not even the magnolia, more beautiful than the orange
tree, when the ripe fruit and the blossoms mingle with
foliage of the deepest green. It was a beautiful conception of the Spaniard to call this the land of the angels.
We will not stop at that ancient seat of our military
power, Fort Yuma, at the crossing of the Colorado, except
to say good-bye to California.

Passing the long line of rail through Arizona and New
Mexico and the giant State of Texas, we reach New Orleans. It was here the illustrious patriot and statesman,
the anniversary of whose natal day we celebrate, achieved
great renown as a warrior. It is one hundred and fifteen
years since the day of his birth and forty-five since his re-
tirement from public life. Yet his name and fame are
cherished with the same devotion by the people as when
in their midst he defended their safety on the battlefield
and protected their rights in the executive mansion.

We stand beside the Father of Waters. He rages, and

his anger is frightful. His punishment of the people on the border is cruel and remorseless. He has broken away from the restraints that held him in the channel. He has driven the people from their farms and seized their lands. What agencies shall be invoked to control the turbulent waters? When it was once my duty to speak and vote on this question, I had difficulty in satisfying myself of the authority of Congress to vote money to maintain the levees. It seemed it was not so much in aid of commerce as to defend and protect agriculture. But I came to the conclusion that as Jefferson had found authority in the Constitution for the purchase of that country, I might feel authorized to vote for its preservation. The great interests of the country require it.

Shall we return by Washington? Perhaps it would be of interest to witness something of the strife between the belligerent Republican party. My sympathies were with the stalwarts. I thought them the more sincere and honest; and also they seemed to be the "under dog in the fight."

Our journey is now ended. What have we observed? This we can say: Our country is great and strong because it has a great and strong population. We have journeyed among the people and observed their characteristics. Engaged in useful and honorable industry, they fill the valleys; seeking homes, subsistence and wealth, they climb the mountain sides.

The great qualities that characterize our people are the result, as I suppose, of the commingling of the blood of the strongest nations. They are irresistible in the pursuits of peace, invincible in war. Barbarism in Russia and cruelty in England will stimulate the spirit of immigration to these States from all parts of Europe, and our population will be increased at a greater ratio than ever.

We have also observed in our journey the great variety of climate, of soil, and of production; each section is developing those industries to which it is best adapted. You gentlemen who have never before traveled over the great Northwest have seen with wonder and admiration the extent and value of our agricultural productions, while we of the North have rejoiced at the increased cotton growth of the South.

We all rejoice in the fact that the sections maintain an honorable and friendly rivalry for the greatest success in their respective productions. Cotton in the South and corn in the North each claims to be king. They are so great, so powerful, and contribute so largely to hold the balance of trade in our favor with other countries, that each may well claim a scepter. In excellence of quality and the quantity produced, each has almost the exclusive product of this country, and each may securely rely upon the wants of mankind to supply a market. That product which always commands a market is king.

Mr. Chairman and gentlemen, while with gratified pride we are considering the vast extent of our country and the great variety and enormous value of its productions, we are admonished that the purest of our patriots and the wisest of our statesmen have expressed their fears and profound anxiety lest out of these shall come jealousies and antagonisms. No danger need be apprehended from that source if we but stand by our system and form of government. It was the child of patriotism and wisdom, and experience has proven it well suited to our condition. It is madness to hope that a consolidated and single authority can maintain peaceful government over a country so extended, and with productions and interests so varied. If we but maintain the constitutional authority of the United States, and preserve to each State the right to regulate whatever belongs to itself alone, we fear no troubles arising from sectional jealousies, however much our territory may be extended or our productions increased.

"ANDREW JACKSON."

Response by Hon. William F. Vilas, of Wisconsin, at a banquet of the Iroquois Club, at Chicago, March 15, 1882.

Mr. President and Gentlemen of the Iroquois Club:

The selection of this anniversary for your first festival is a signal mark of the patriotism, wisdom and political courage which animate your organization, and a prophecy of its usefulness.

Andrew Jackson! What a flood of glorious history rises on the name! A generation ago and more, the old Democratic hero passed behind the curtain of death, but only in the flesh to die! The mortal change was his apotheosis to the celestial company of the gods of our political religion.

Well worthy of his immortality was that heroic life. Riven by passion and scarred by the strokes of strife, yet it stands a colossal figure among the heroes and statesmen of mankind, pre-eminent for single-hearted honesty of purpose and exalted bravery to do and bear.

The ivy of affection and the laurel of renown, rich by the growth of years, now hide beneath their beauty the scars and seams of human weakness in that splendid tower of God's architecture in man. The features of its majesty and strength alone are left open to view. Turn we our gaze on them, behold the beacon which blazes from its lofty head, and fitly celebrate his day by invoking the inspiration of that character to rule again our political world.

This country ever loved, and, as it shall be ever free, ever must love, in its true ideal, the Jackson Democracy. False leadership and the turbulence of war distracted its counsels, obscured its distinctiveness and scattered its followers among various parties. The painful political scenes of our day cry aloud for their patriotic reunion and the restoration of its power.

It was not great intellect which made Andrew Jackson

a great leader of men. It was his towering character. He had great intellect, and for war genius. But high above all, as mountain peaks ascend above the lower lying hills, rose the lofty eminences of his stupendous character. Its paramount features were indomitable will and daring, but intelligent courage. No page of history tells of one who, before him, survived seventy-eight years and so continually performed such and so many actions of desperate audacity. From early boyhood to whitened age, he was beset by perils and involved in strife, sometimes crippled by wounds and often broken by disease. Others would have yielded, or, not yielding, would have died. But not he! Through every year of life, in every danger, in difficulties unmeasured, the flame of that matchless soul burned undimmed; his courage never flinched, nor his iron will surrendered.

His personal hardihood was not more remarkable than his moral courage. The two went hand in hand. He as boldly met the judgment of men and angels as the efforts of an enemy. For he was founded on absolute honesty of thought. Not always right, he always thought he was right. His acts were sometimes wrong; his purposes in them to his mind never. It guided him in quarrels with his enemies, it ennobled his intercourse with friends. It governed his individual transactions, and rose to exaltation when he dealt for his country and fellow men. There his example voiced the teaching: The man is a felon who in politics cheats the people, and he a traitor who betrays public trust.

And this our day and generation, which has seen a secret plotter, because his corrupt arts turned awry a State's election on which a Presidential contest pivoted, wined and feasted as a political hero—which witnesses even now at the capital of its greatest State the consummation of a shameful compact for the barter of public offices of trust—while yet we have not ceased to shudder from the horror of a President's assassination in time of peace, because of the passionate intrigues of faction—may well return an anxious eye to the lesson of honest conviction and integrity of purpose taught by Jackson's open war. Better far to the country were all his upright errors than a single drop of the subtle poison of the blood innoculated by the chicane and fraud which have been too long the instruments of power in the Republic.

These were the qualities which made the leadership of Jackson great and successful. , These magnetized and unified the Jackson Democracy of fifty years ago. These were their principles of action—first, to see the right, blazing with the authority of the burning bush to Moses, then fight for it, recking no peril.

Above all, and first of all, the Jackson Democrat, as Jackson did, loves his country with a love which knows no higher duty but to God. He loves this complex frame of government which, when young, kings derided, and the world cannot comprehend this mystic child of Liberty, heaven-conceived, of one in many and many in one; this fast-bound Union of Independent States, this system of the stars, resting on the equipoise of contending forces, safe as law and free as space. He loves it without reasoning and with reason; not alone because it shelters his wife and babes and household gods, protects his labor and opens unlimited possibilities to his manhood; but because it satisfies the natural longings of his soul, because our fathers won it as the price of blood, because it is the ark of their covenant and holds in security the fruit and hope of Liberty. He loves it because it stands up in the way of the tyrants of the earth; inviting the oppressed to safety and teaching the example of freedom to men. The springing manhood of his youth rejoices in this idol, superior to the love of woman, and the experience of his age sinks the roots of his affection in wisdom and philanthropy.

Such was Jackson's patriotism, intense as his character, passionate and true. It was a nursling of the bloody Tarleton's Waxhaw massacre, printed on his boyish head by a British butcher's sword-stroke, nourished in captivity while yet but fourteen. It sank deep in his heart as he helped to raise the frame of a State in the wilds of primitive Tennessee, and fought the savage in the Southern glades and forests. And how full of glory to his country were its ripened fruits! Recall the scenes of the second war with Great Britain. With all our victories on lake and sea, disaster and humiliation had befallen us by land. Our soil had been invaded, our capital captured and ravaged by fire. Our wide seacoast, so promising to commerce, seemed helpless of defense. And when England gathered at Jamaica her vast armada, boastfully threatening to seize our great river, rob us of our new-bought territory, and push her ships and armies northward, till her cordon of empire bound us from Canada to the Gulf, who compared her mighty preparations with our feeble force, without some fear? Who but Andrew Jackson? With the daring patriotism of Leonidas, intelligently skillful as it was desperate, he flung, by night, his little band upon the enemy, instantly he had landed upon the Louisiana shore; then, gaining delay to raise a hasty breastwork, with bloody slaughter of her trained and veteran army, he gave to England, more by valor than by arms, her most ignominious defeat, and, changing our humiliation to joy, finished the war in glory by the splendid victory of New Orleans.

Not alone by a savage or a foreign enemy was that love of country tried. When his hair was white with the toils and wars of more than three-score years, when care, disease and grief had long pressed hard upon his soul, from the very people he had fought and labored for, from his own Southern clime a deadly blow was leveled at his country. The treason of secession raised its horrid front to defy the Constitution and tear our Union asunder. Though many trembled, the old President was unshaken. With the fierce alacrity of youth, he met it before it came forward; and raising that fitting cry of a Republic's Chief Magistrate, "By the God of Heaven I will uphold the laws," he struck the treason down!

He knew but one dealing with his country's enemy, whether he came in ships across the sea, or traitorously at home struck at the sacred bond of Union; to fight him on the instant and to fight him to the death.

And this is the devotion everywhere of the true Jackson Democrat. This led him to the fore-ranks of war, when a second time secession aimed its mortal stroke upon our nation's bond, when, alas! no Jackson stood in front. Forgotten all divisions, loosed all other ties, this devotion bound the Jackson Democrat to all true comrades in arms. Let the warriors who fought with tongues and offices, at home, raise their chatter in vain! It was not they! This fellowship of the brave in patriotic duty then saved the Republic to men, and shall be its safe foundation forever!

Fellow Democrats! These were the ruling guides of the illustrious man whose name and inspiration you invoke to-night. But volumes only can tell the many deeds and services by which he exemplified them in action. I may not pause to touch them with even bare allusion.

Yet I would bid you mark his dealings with another peculiar danger to popular institutions—the clutch of a great corporation on the Government. Like other combinations of capital, the Bank of the United States had its field and day of usefulness. In its useful work it was entitled to credit and protection, and both it received. But with strength it grew ambitious, and strained for unjust power. It stretched out its arm and took the Congress in its grasp. It defied the Executive, and a weaker one would have bent to its will. But Jackson smote it, like

Hercules the dragon, and it fell! And with it fell to us the warning: Keep corporations in their places. Hands off the government of the free!

And still more pertinent to the day is it to recall his entrance on the field of national politics. Then, as now, a vicious party system bound the people and fettered their free choice. Spurning the power of the caucus, he burst its bands of false cohesion as a mass of cobweb, and won the people overwhelmingly by direct, open war. Let us emulate the pregnant example. Down with intrigues for office! Democracy wants no hireling soldiery who war for sack and spoil! Up with the clear-cut principles which mark the manhood of a free man, and recruit our hosts from them who will fight for the right because it is right—for love of country and fellow-men.

There is work enough to do, were we all herculean. The Augean stables must be cleaned of long-accumulated corruption; our public trusts set utterly above the reach of political beasts of prey; our trade made free of taxes which rob the general public; our commerce to ride the waves of every sea, beneath our country's flag.

Fill up, then, gentlemen, a brimming cup to the glorious memory of Andrew Jackson. With joy all good men may drink it through the reunited nation. In Southern homes his name must have peculiar honor. For he was theirs from whom we claim this heritage of glory! And so was the majestic Washington! So was Jefferson! And a long line of sacred memory! Well may they jump the sins of a later generation to sink in oblivion, and seize again on the traditions of the fathers as theirs and ours together. Drink to the glories of the past—the hopes of coming time! And, while this government bears the ark of liberty down the ages, green grow the laurels on the hero's grave and sweetly rest his sleep! Abide with us forever the alert and fearless courage, the open simple honesty, and pure, patriotic love of Old Hickory!

"BUSINESS EDUCATION AND EDUCATION AMONG BUSINESS MEN; A MORE THOROUGH GENERAL EDUCATION IS ESSENTIAL TO THE AMERICAN MERCHANT, IN ORDER THAT HE MAY SUCCESSFULLY PROSECUTE THE GREAT AFFAIRS OF COMMERCE, AND HAPPILY ENJOY THE FRUITS OF HIS LABOR."

Response by Col. W. F. Vilas, of Madison, Wis., at a banquet of the Milwaukee Merchants' Association, June 5, 1884.

Mr. President and Gentlemen:

The sentiment rather invites an essay than a speech; a studious, passionless, and extensive excursion upon a wide domain of history and thought. It is a serious theme, full of interest and value, and that you set it forward for prominent contemplation in this joyous hour of festivity, testifies the honorable spirit which rules the merchants of Wisconsin's metropolis. The craving for broader education is the proof of enlightenment already gained in great degree; it bespeaks a mind already educated to comprehension of our nature, and conscious of its capability for exalted power and exquisite pleasure; it is the noble appetite of the soul. And the reflection is pleasing to us, members of the brotherhood of Liberty, that everywhere in our happy land, from every calling, from all the ranks of business and of labor, mercantile, professional and mechanical, that yearning cry is heard, marking steady diffusion of intelligence, enlarged appreciation of the power of knowledge, increased numbers set free in intellect by their free equality in law. The lamp of science now bestows its rays on every scene of human effort, and the quickening power of its light stimulates inquiry and growth in every field where industry adds some product for the comfort or joy of men. The teeming mouth of the mine is vocal with the sounds of inventive science; the forest, in rapid fall, reverberates its mighty stroke; the farmside mingles the melody of civilization's machinery with nature's voices; and, in various form, the manufactory hums the notes of enlightened progress. New methods constantly grant greater forces to man; multiply the old and develop new products to enter the marts of trade.

The merchant is the agent and factor of all the ranks of industry and life; gathering from every class, distributing to every class. He must be quick to know the wants of all, the availability of the products of all. At his highest value, he must advantageously partake the knowledge of all. His intelligence must comprehend not only the necessities, but the luxuries, the elegant tastes, the most delicate gratifications. He teaches the producer what are the choicest demands of society, the consumer what the richest fruits of labor. Nor will the jealous exaction of an ambitious people suffer the American merchant to limit his trials to his own country. He has ever been, and must not cease to be, the adventurous traveler of the globe. And now a thousand avenues are opened, and new journeyings inviting him, where, but shortly since, comparatively few challenged his attempts. The railroad and steamship have made all the produce of earth his commodities, every clime his garden, every people his customers. His ear must catch the daily notes of traffic, thrumming the electric wire from every leading mart of trade around the great world. His factors must be in Europe, in China, in the Indies, in South America, in the northern seas, and the far-off islands of the great oceans, and his competition outstrip rivals in every land and clime. Wherever on earth the want of his country's productions is to be discovered or excited, there his penetrating activity must find a market. Alert, enterprising, indefatigable, bold, handling every product of scientific industry or popular need, rapping at the gate of every avenue of commerce—such the character and mission which a great people demand of the American merchant. Well may you say the most extensive education is essential to his successful prosecution of the great affairs of commerce committed to his charge.

For, not alone must the merchant intimately know the methods and the articles of production, the channels of intercourse, the varied wants and the changing markets of the people of the earth; he must know the science of applied statistics, the laws of trade and political economy —whence comes the wisdom to forecast events, and, still more, he must be a lawyer—in several languages—to read the chart of artificial reefs and obstructed channels by which the statutes of different nations, according to the respective degrees of their ignorance, prejudice and self-wounding selfishness, imperil the rich argosies of commerce.

But no further here. Politics is barred.

True it is, minute and skillful division of these vast labors apportions but a minor share to the individual. But this is also true of every great department of affairs, and not otherwise could great achievements follow. It argues no less intelligence to be necessary to the class; it detracts nothing from the magnitude and credit of the common enterprise. The highest rank in any calling can be reached only by possession of the gifts and acquirements requisite to perform its functions; and the noblest aim and effort lead honorably to the foremost place. Whosoever is unwilling to undergo the conditions of a higher, must take, in contentment, his lesser place; who looks to be a leader among American merchants, must be equipped with the knowledge of the world. A broader and a truer education is also needful in another point of view—to enforce the policy of honesty, and guard against the wild irruptions of folly. It must be confessed the time has not yet passed when Darien colonization schemes, South Sea bubbles, and Mississippi companies, in other guises and by other names, may sink the earnings of a generation. Business men still sometimes mistake reckless speculation for business, and seek the road to wealth "across lots." Is it not true, for some time past, much of our legitimate traffic has been a mere body-servant to gambling? When the lexicon of business is chiefly studied for definition of "puts," "calls," "spreads," and "straddles;" when the neophyte is taught to buy what is not sold, and to sell what he does not own, "business education" is a direct preparation for the faro-table or sweat-cloth. For years Wall street and Monaco might have been indifferently visited for "business," with equal morality, and the former has been infinitely more pernicious in consequences. It has spread the fatal itch among the people, which, long hid in the circulation, is now broken out in recent mortgages, pock-spotting the whole country. That is, I understand, the healthy state of eruptive disease; and it may be hoped our period of convalescence has begun. It demands educated intelligence to distinguish and guide the daring enterprises of honest business which bring legitimate gains, though often large, especially, to commend to the man of moderate affairs the wisdom of patience, the security and certainty of that steady growth which builds the oak by yearly rings of gain; above all, to shun the seductive lures of dishonest speculation, which, sooner or later, surely wrecks its inebriated victim.

It is a special pleasure to touch another feature of your toast. Happy, indeed, is that enjoyment of the fruits of labor which derives its zest from the accomplishments of the mind. This bodily frame, in youth exuberant with expanding powers, advances in growth but to manhood's middle age; then begins its slow, its swift descent to mortal dissolution, tortured with a thousand ills, monitory of the end. Not so the mind. Rightly guided, its faculties develop, its tastes improve, its wisdom strengthens, and all its pleasures widen, from when the body begins to fail; and, not rarely, the soul shows its climax of nobility as it shakes off the mortal dust. But there is an inexorable condition. Unremitting and generous cultivation alone bestows these treasures. Wealth of intellect, like the honest fortune of industry, is the fruit of patient accumulation, the slow product of wisdom and philosophy. The appetites of youth pall in age; the more bitterly, the greater the youthful indulgence. Woe betide that man whose only resource for joy has been their gratification, when the ills of age beset him! Hardly less pitiable is he whom a sordid greed enslaves. He stands like some solitary trunk, when the fire has swept the forest; every leaf and flower turned to blackness, where nature offered a scene of beauty. It is the peculiar peril of the man of business, who must needs employ his faculties for gain. Well shall it be for him if he wisely applies in time the counter-check of polite studies. Happily falls the eventide of life on that man, who, with a garnered competence, has secured his quiet seat where the sun-rays of philosophy and literature shall soften, with delicious colors, the twilight of his declining day; and sweetly shall his natural sleep embrace him at its close. There is, in the volumes of recorded lore, a mine of interest and delight for the special delectation of the merchant-student.

It has been, perhaps still is, an affectation of the so-called nobility across the sea, to contemn the man of trade, calling all—in scorn—shopkeepers; and even servile scholars—for mere learning never gave independence —have stalked along behind, carrying the train of this pride. You may, at times, chance to see some blood-cursed heir of this depravity turn up an aristocratic nose —often over a hungry mouth—at bare thought of such association. It is a mushroom of ignorance. Review of the history and deeds of his calling may justly fill the merchant's heart with generous pride.

At its head has stood, from the earliest years of the

race, the genius of inquiry and enterprise. It has been the forlorn hope and the vanguard of civilization. In ancient days, when priests and scholars turned for knowledge their feeble gaze to the stars, in credulous lunacy, and every stranger was a frightful barbarian and a foe, the merchant's caravan unfolded a knowledge of the earth and of the arts of life. In later times, when the deluge of barbarism had submerged the civilization of the ancients, and again darkness was upon the face of the earth, the rays of returning light shone from the cities which the Adriatic merchant built and endowed, and thence, also, sprung that perfect code of the laws of business, to which all civilization pays the grateful tribute of obedience. Afterwards, when tyrants, big and small, ruled and robbed the land of Europe; while pirates despoiled the seas, alike unchecked by fear of justice or of a spiritless and subjugated people, it was the merchants and tradesmen who joined together that puissant league of towns which bowed princes to their law, strung pirates to their gibbets, and taught the first lessons to the people of their rights and power. It was little Holland, mighty in her knowledge of the laws of trade, from whose mercantile genius, like Minerva from the head of Jove, sprung Grotius, to write that law which rules nations as its subjects; it was trading Holland which gave secure asylum to the oppressed in conscience, and ushered from its shores the adventurous pilgrims, heralds of liberty to the new world.

It has been the merchant who broke the synonymy of enemy and stranger, who discovered the brotherhood of man, and pioneered the civilization which Christianity purified; it was the merchant who practiced the Baconian philosophy before Bacon lived, and displayed, by his adventurous inquiry, the beginning of many sciences; it was the merchant whose intelligent courage and wisdom first subdued the anarchy, that broke the tyranny of the middle ages, and gave the spirit of liberty to the land, and all the security of law to the sea.

And as we stand here in the mere youth-time of a new and mighty world, may we not strain a prophetic eye to that future day when the American merchant—worthy inheritor of the glories of his line—descending to his ships from either shore of this harmonious continent, shall cause the gigantic arteries of an earth-surrounding traffic to beat from the American heart of commerce, concentrating here the returning wealth of all nations.

"OUR HOTEL—John Plankinton's house, the famous Caravansary of the Northwest; grand in its proportions and in all its appointments, they simply reflect the head and heart of its originator and proprietor—one of Milwaukee's foremost citizens."

Response by James G. Jenkins, at a banquet of the Milwaukee Merchants' Association, June 5, 1884.

Mr. President:

The theme assigned me is double; the house Plankinton, and the man Plankinton. Ordinarily—like a patent of nobility—they speak for themselves; they are their own best advocates. It seems, however, fitting to the time when the merchants of Milwaukee hold their annual feast, sacred to their titular deity Ceres, the goddess of corn and of harvests, and appropriate to the occasion when they dedicate to use this beautiful banquet hall, that mention should be made of the house that is the pride of the city, and of the man whose public spirit has made such an hostelry an accomplished fact.

The practical religion of a practical age declares as infallible truth that man's first great duty is to his stomach. Unless that organ be healthful and well supplied, the body is not nourished, the brain works awry, and dis-

torted fancies usurp the throne of reason and of common
sense. The ill-conditioned stomach can neither rightly
appreciate the present life, nor justly reason on the life
to come. In vain the missionary appeals to the starving
savage to comprehend and reconcile the great fundamental doctrines of predestination, election, fore-ordination
and free-will. But fill that empty stomach with whole-
some food, and the brain receives invigorating force, sufficient, if the treatment be timely prosecuted, to digest
even those theological brick-bats. The communist is
merely a starving stomach crying for food, the protest of
nature's law of nourishment against man's law of starva-
tion; forcible the protest, because the demands of nature
are peremptory; violent, because to the starving, peaceable means seem unavailing. A full stomach is, politically, conservative. An ill-fed stomach is radical in proportion to its emptiness. The safety of the state lies not
in written constitutions, nor in armies, but in well-filled
stomachs. The bullet of wheat is more effective than the
bullet of lead.

> "Let me have men about me that are fat;
> Sleek-headed men, and such as sleep o'nights;
> Yond' Cassius has a lean and hungry look;
> He thinks too much; such men are dangerous."

In all the progress of the race, man's first effort has
been to better his physical condition. The race has striven
—is still striving—for better homes, for better clothing,
for better food, and, last but not the least, for better cooking. Not, perhaps, to so great an extent as formerly, but
still, in large measure, is it true to-day that "Heaven
sends us good meat, but the devil sends us cooks."

In spite of the wonderful advance in scientific knowledge and the means of information, but little progress,
outside of the commercial centers, has been made in the
science of cooking. Cooking should be one of the learned
professions. It is the master of all. It gives tone to
religious thought. It makes and unmakes presidents. It

largely influences legislation and the administration of
the law. It affects the decision of the judge upon the law,
and the finding of the jury upon the facts. It creates
the necessity which renders tolerable the medical profession. But, sad to say, the science of cooking is for the
most part in the keeping of the ignorant and the careless.
The coat of arms of the average cook should be a weak
concoction of coffee couchant, with a fried beefsteak
rampant.

The cook is man's tyrant. Before this despot how
powerless are we! His sway is all-pervading. He is responsible for most of the evils of life. He may be persuasive also to the attainment of great happiness. Mens sana
in corpore sano—a sound mind in a sound body—is to the
rational mind the indispensable condition of complete
manhood. The one cannot exist without the other, and
both are dependent in a large degree upon the cook. He
controls our destinies, our bodies, our nerves, our
thoughts, our ambitions. His art or want of skill builds
up or destroys the body, enriches or impoverishes the
blood, strengthens or weakens the nerves, affects the very
fibre of the brain, the very quality of thought. The success or failure of "enterprises of great pith and moment"
often hinge upon the quality of one's breakfast. The cook
may be either Vishnu, the preserver, or Siva, the de-
stroyer. He most frequently develops as the latter divinity. He is the fruitful parent of dyspepsia, and dyspepsia
destroys a good statesman, a good merchant, a good lawyer, and a good citizen. The dyspeptic is always a bear—
in more senses than one—and as to every enterprise. The
well-fed stomach looks grandly and hopefully upon life,
its possibilities and its means of usefulness. The English are wise. Their appeals for charitable, religious and
public aid are made at the close of a good dinner. The
subtle chord of sympathy between the stomach and the

pocket-book can only be tuned to sweet music by the cook.

This tyrant of ours is unassailable—entrenched in power. His government is an absolute despotism, accompanied by heavy taxation without much representation. There is no republican form of government in the kitchen. No revolution can dethrone him, and we cannot live without our tyrant. Although he slay us, yet must we trust in him.

> "We may live without poetry, music and art;
> We may live without conscience, and live without heart;
> We may live without friends; we may live without books;
> But civilized man cannot live without cooks."

Seeing, then, that much of life depends upon the cook, that the stability of governments and the destinies of men are within his power, ought we not, as lovers of our country and of our fellows, to seek the application of the principles of good government first where it is most needed— to the kitchen? We have common schools all over the land to nourish the brain. Let us have cooking schools to nourish the body. Let the rallying cry be, "Shall the coming woman cook?" It matters little whether Arthur or Blaine, or Tilden or Cleveland be president. It is essential to the safety of the republic that we inaugurate true civil-service reform in the kitchen. Some one has said that "if a man were permitted to make all the ballads, he need not care who should make the laws of a nation." Let Plankinton name the cooks, and I will show you better ballads and better laws.

The contrast between the ancient inn and the modern hotel presents in striking manner the progress of civilization.

Anciently, stringent laws were necessary to protect the guest from the landlord. The latter was usually poor, of rather unsavory reputation, and sometimes a highwayman. Being unable—like the modern landlord—to absorb all of his guests' money in a legal way, he resorted to forcible and unlawful measures to obtain it. The inn of the olden time was a necessity to furnish a meagre livelihood to the landlord. The hotel of a commercial metropolis now is the plaything of a millionaire. Formerly, traveling, even for short distances from home, was confined to the rich, and was infrequent. The inn, therefore, was adapted only to the needs of the time. It was small and crude in all its appointments, and yet it must have furnished a deal of comfort; for a century ago, so great a man as Samuel Johnson asserted, that "there is nothing which has yet been contrived by man by which so much happiness is produced as by a good tavern or inn." But so great have become the means of communication in modern times, and so confirmed the necessity and habit of frequent and long journeys, that the inn has, at all commercial centers, developed into a palace, attended by an army of retainers, quick to meet the requirements of the guest. Royalty in the time of Elizabeth was not lodged or fed as is the ordinary American sovereign in the modern inn. A ducal palace in all its glory could not compare with a metropolitan hotel of to-day. It is magnificent in its proportions, royal in its appointments, epicurean in its larder, luxurious in all its surroundings. The modern inn is a sure indication of the progress of the race in material wealth and physical comfort.

And now to come back to my text. Of all modern hotels there are doubtless many that are larger, but I think none can surpass in quiet, but beautiful and rich interior, in attention and care for guests, the fullness, richness and variety of its larder, in the whiteness and cleanliness of its linen, and the solid comfort of its beds, in the excellency of its cooking, the Plankinton House of Milwaukee. All that art and science and money could supply, has been supplied, and with no niggard hand, to render this an abode of luxurious ease. Beautiful marbles and frescoes delight the eye. Here sweet, clean beds invite to repose. Here every comfort is at your bidding. The "salted seas," the great lakes and the mountain streams yield their rich food. The forests and the great prairies render their savory game. The tropics and the Pacific slope bestow delicious fruits. The tables groan beneath the weight of luxury And here is a cook upon whom the title is rightly bestowed. He is an artist, not a boor. He knows better than to fry a steak, and can discern the difference between coffee and dishwater. And there is a bar—ah, gentlemen, I see your eyes glisten and mouths water at the very mention of the place—a bar where the choicest beverages, the most fragrant Havanas, are at command. There every taste may be gratified. There is champagne for the man of high license, Best's beer for the man of low license, and an excellent quality of Apollinaris for the prohibitionist.

In brief, whatever of luxury unlimited means can command, with respect to the lodgment and care of guests, can here be found. With John Plankinton as general in command, and Charles W. White as brigadier, the guest may always be assured of right royal welcome and right royal care.

Well may Milwaukee be proud of the Plankinton—house and man. Fitting is it that the merchants of the city should dedicate this elegant banquet room. Here hold your annual feasts; for many a day shall pass before Milwaukee can boast a finer room, a more elegant hotel, a more sumptuous table, or better cooking than we have seen and enjoyed to-night.

Of the man Plankinton—to whom the city and state are indebted for this noble hostelry—it is needless to speak in any mere words of praise. To say of him that his name is a synonym of honor, of large-hearted liberality, of enlightened public spirit, is but to say what is a proverb with every man, woman and child in Milwaukee. The monuments of his enterprise and public liberality are seen and known of all. His private charities are known only to the recipients. Long may he live to enjoy the well-deserved esteem of his neighbors, and the fruits of an honest and well-spent life.

I conclude, Mr. President, by asking leave to propose the health of John Plankinton,

The sagacious merchant,

The public-spirited citizen,

The friend of the poor,

The Christian gentleman,

The man who "can keep a hotel."

" THE JURY."

Response by George W. Wakefield, at the banquet of the Iowa State Bar Association, at Davenport, Iowa, July 38, 1896.

The jury is an ancient and honorable branch of the court, a safeguard to personal liberty, fostered and preserved by a freedom-loving people, and the direct legacy of the common law to us. It is essentially democratic in its origin and nature and grew out of the customs and laws of a people who in the savage and barbarous state acknowledged no king. Then the sovereign communities were small, the members of each few, and the whole body of freemen in each, assembled full armed, in their annual court, when officers for the year were elected, public business transacted and the more grave controversies between individuals as well as offenses against the community, were heard and determined by the voice of all. This simple method has grown and changed with the increase in numbers, the combination of small communities into great states, and the advance of civilization and consequent increasing complexity of controversies. The forming of a great state made a representative system for the small communities necessary, not only in the ordinary affairs of government, but also in the determination of controversies. The Anglo-Saxon, carried to England from the German forests, the court of the hundred and the wapentake, where all the people attended. As numbers increased it was found inconvenient to require all to attend the Shire courts, and provision was made for a specified number from each hundred as "the four best men," to attend instead. So through representation by slow steps has grown the jury as we now have it. In its scope and purpose the jury is representative of the people, and when untrammeled its influence is on the side of personal right and popular privilege and opposed to prerogative and kingly tyranny. Monarchs do not look upon it with kindly eyes. While the infamous Jeffreys coerced the jury to find Alice Lisle guilty of high treason, another jury, notwithstanding the influence of the king, acquitted the seven bishops who refused to aid James II. to overthrow the Protestant faith. Though the jury that acquitted Sir Nicholas Throgmorton in disregard of the wishes of the judges were assessed to pay enormous fines by the council in the Star Chamber, yet in the face of threatened punishment a jury found William Penn not guilty of an offense for having spoken at a Quaker meeting. A jury relieved the Virginia planters from the undue burden of a tobacco tax, though all the influence of prerogative was used to enforce that burden. The jury system had no place upon the continent of modern Europe until it was introduced by the French Revolution. Since then it has been quite generally adopted in some form and with various limitations for the trial of the more grave criminal causes, but it has not been used in determining civil matters, the continental jurists thinking the system not well adapted to such use. One of the French jurists has well said: "Of all the positions of trust which the law can confer on a citizen, there is not one which requires more of discernment, of independence and of real morality, than that of juryman; and a study of the political movements and reforms on the continent of Europe for the past century will show the profound interest which the jury has excited there, while the number of laws that have been enacted with a view to bringing good men into the jury box and regulating their actions according to the best principles, testifies to the fact that the author above quoted but voices a general conviction." (Dr. Scaife.)

In 1864 the jury system obtained a foothold in Russia, the land of absolute monarchy. While the system is thus growing and extending over continental Europe, it is with us growing more and more common to hear disparaging remarks about the jury and our jury system. There may be just cause of complaint as to the particulars of our jury system and its workings as now constituted. If so, then the people should by apt laws remedy the defect and not destroy the system. There is no perfect human law, and the best human ingenuity can devise will only approximately secure right and justice among men. Those laws best considered and best adapted to the purposes intended and most generally accepted in particular cases, sometimes result in hardship. If the results are uncertain, so are all human judgments. Are the judgments of Chancery Courts more easy to forecast than the verdict of the jury? Richard Francis, more than a hundred years ago, said it was a common objection that courts of equity were uncertain and precarious, and the unhappy suitor must enter such court with doubts and fears. Whether the conditions have improved, each may answer for himself if the number of appeals and reversals do not answer it for him. As the old English king made the length of his arm the standard length of the English ell, so monarchs and rulers are still disposed to insist that their conscience is the measure of good and evil, and justice can only proceed from them in the business affairs of everyday life. However, the fact is that there is no perfect human judgment or conscience. The men of science, trained to thought and deliberate study, watching the heavens night after night through the telescope, find that their observations of the same body at the

same time do not agree, and through extended comparison
of many observations by a corps of observers they compute
and assign to each his tendency to error, which is called
personal equation, and which is considered as inhering in
all of his observations. So we, men of the law, as well as
men of the business world and ordinary jurors, each and all
have our personal equation, but we have not, like the men
of science, by extensive comparison, measured and determined what it is. Duport, advocating the introduction of
the jury system into France, said: "Every man can be used
for unearthing a fact." We cannot in this age and time use
every man. The multitude of causes and necessities of civil
life forbid. Many are by nature or by want of education
ill adapted to such service generally, and their personal
equation is so great as to render their use undesirable. It
is therefore wise to impose restrictions in selecting jurors,
so that the more capable can be chosen. Jurors selected
with reasonable care from the various walks of life, having
due regard to character and judgment, will each present in
the jury room some personal equation, some tendency to
error, but these tendencies will vary with the individuals,
and each will in some measure offset and modify the other
so that the joint personal equation of the twelve men will
be minimized in the verdict. In Iowa the recent jury law
was framed to carry out the thought of Duport and to make
all voters in turn serve upon the jury. The law makes the
jury thoroughly representative. It brought into the jury
box all classes and conditions, indifferent and bad jurors
as well as good ones, and no doubt, in some localities, the
change from a system of selected names as eligible jurymen, was a change for the worse. It is desirable that the
list of eligible jurymen should be as extensive and as thoroughly representative as reasonable care can make it, but
with such limitations that it may not be truly said:

> "The jury passing on the prisoner's life,
> May in the sworn twelve, have a thief or two
> Guiltier than him they try."

The present jury laws may need modification and be capable of improvement, but in its essential character the jury should remain a permanent institution in all free governments, for it is the best system devised by man for the trial of criminal causes and issues of fact involving conflict of testimony.

> "For men's judgments are
> A parcel of their fortunes; and all things outward
> Do draw the inward quality after them."

" OUR COUNTRY."

Response by Hon. Thos. F. Bayard, of Delaware, at a banquet of the Iroquois Club, at Chicago, April 13, 1883.

Mr. Chairman and Gentlemen of the Iroquois Club:

The toast you have just given is surely the best in the world to bring an American a thousand miles to respond to it, and no better place for such response can be found than this proudly representative city of Chicago—so distinctively American—where the pulsations of energy, enterprise, and feeling are so full, warm and strong, and the characteristics of our country so splendidly illustrated. And in what assemblage can such a theme be more properly contemplated and discussed than that in which I happily find myself to-night? For I see around me a group of my fellow-countrymen, called together from private occupations by a common impulse of patriotic observance and commemoration, animated by a public spirit, seeking only to promote the cause of good government and the prosperity of all classes through the organization of a political party as the only efficient means to the great end—the regulation and control of all the elements to society by a system of laws enacted and forms ordained for self-government by the people—a government of a great family of republics, each exercising for itself, and within its borders, the essential rights, and fulfilling the correspondent duties of local self-government, and all bound in a union for a common defense

and the general welfare under a written constitution of delegated and limited powers.

The topic you have selected is the highest, our place of
meeting the fittest, this assemblage the most congenial, and
the occasion, the 143rd anniversary of the birth of the illustrious author of the declaration of American independence,
"The title-deed of the liberties of the American people."

Do not suppose that I am so unmindful of the proprieties
of the occasion, or so ungrateful as to requite your hospitali-
ties by a long recital of statistics of the wealth and progress
of this country. What I have to say shall be said shortly.

Grand as is our own heritage, magnificent and marvelous as is the landed estate which we call "our country,"
it is its soul rather than its body, the jewel rather than the
casket containing it, which attracts my thought to-night,
and impels me to invite yours. And yet a glance at this
grand empire of land and sea, upon whose sides break the
waves of two oceans, over whose fair and ample bosom
countless rivers thread their way, like veins carrying life-
blood and fructification for the millions who gather strength
and subsistence from such exuberant fountains of supply,
may imperfectly disclose the material force—the actual extent of the land so bounteously given to us for our own use
for life, and in remainder to our posterity forever.

For, in the language of Webster, "We are in the line
of conveyance through which, whatever has been obtained
by the spirit and efforts of our ancestors, is to be communi-
cated to our children."

With no desire to inflate national vanity, it may not be
uninstructive to take a glance over this vast unbroken area
of our dominions, almost four millions of square miles, an
acreage staggering to arithmetical expression; with a present population of 55,000,000, and increased by an annual
immigration of nearly one million; with climate infinite in
its variety, soils teeming with every vegetable production
known to man's imagination or needed for his use; mines

of every metal, precious and base; a land so vast in extent, so varied in feature, so replete in all that can elevate and gratify human feeling and imagination, or exalt the sense of religious gratitude; within whose borders a lifetime could well be spent in travel and discovery, to find at its close that but a fragment of the great whole had been seen, and its marvelous capacities and beauties scarcely comprehended.

Standing thus upon the highlands of vision, realizing the material forces placed in our care, how important, how dignified, becomes the duties of each American citizen! How vast the interests committed to his charge! For we cannot disguise the presence nor lessen the weight upon the members of a democratic republic, of individual as well as collective responsibilities to administer well and wisely the affairs of so great an empire, so vast a body of human interests.

And the soul of our country is the spirit of justice and liberty, finding expression under equal laws, for the preservation of which the written Constitution of our Union was ordained, and the free institutions of our government founded.

Left free and unfettered to proclaim and assert themselves, the intelligence and faculties of mankind have vindicated by their results in this country the wisdom of non-interference by the government, either to assist or obstruct the exercise of individual effort and faculty, under regulation of equal laws, in just such mode and direction as the possession of conscious power and inclination by the individual should instruct.

Hence, we have seen in America the children of obscurity and poverty growing strong in their contests with adversity, which elsewhere would have proved an insuperable bar, but, under the equity of our American system, become guides and instructors to success—tests for growing abilities, and encouragements to high and honorable aspirations.

The enduring greatness of our country is founded upon

what is really elevated and great in the minds and hearts of our people. Let us never forget that we have embarked our hopes upon trust—and not upon distrust—in human nature; upon what it contains of strength and worth, and not upon its weakness and depravity; upon the belief that the instinct of self-preservation, left free to recoil from natural and necessary errors and mistakes, will not repeat them; and that, with free and recurrent opportunities for popular elections, misconduct in rulers and mistakes in public policies can and will be corrected and remedied, under the peaceful, orderly and effective forms of law.

And can we be mistaken in the present indications so manifest and abundant, that we are soon to witness, in the election of 1884, a splendid and potential proof of popular wisdom and power to redress grievances, reform unwise policies, rebuke corruption, and purify and strengthen popular institutions; by driving out of the temple of our liberties the mercenary and machine politicians who have betrayed popular trust and disgraced and degraded the administration of our government?

Gentlemen, the era which includes our lifetime is one of remarkable, almost incredible, combination of the results of invention in production of material wealth, in the rapid and facile distribution of that wealth, and the bringing of the whole world into such close and intimate relation that all former conditions of human intercourse are changed, and problems bewildering in number and importance are presented to our view.

Time and space are no longer obstructions to the world's intercourse. The telephone has already brought the lips of New York close against the ear of Chicago, and to "girdle the earth in forty minutes" would be to-day an unpardonable waste of time.

Never in human history was the creation of material wealth so easy, and so marvelously abundant. Its consolidation, under the forms of incorporation, is creating vast units of power which result in monopolies, and absorb and overthrow individual and independent rivalries. Herein are dangers it will behoove us gravely to contemplate, and consider what forces shall be summoned to counteract them. The great question which attends this creation of wealth is: What will you do with it?

Are we to be content with making this land of ours one great wealth-factory? Is that to be the all and end all? Are we to travel over the same lowlands of luxury, effeminacy, corruption and decay as the nations and governments that have risen and fallen before us on the plains of history?

On what do we build, and for what do we build? What greatness do we seek to achieve? To what do our institutions tend?

Is it the creation of mere wealth? or is it the advancement and elevation of the human race? Shall we not light up our pathway of progress as a people with more of justice, more of benevolence, more of the higher attributes that stir within our hearts and dignify our manhood?

The Greek called man anthropos—"one with face turned upward." And what shall be the use of all our wealth-creating inventions if they do not turn man's face upward, and create a higher range of personal feeling, ambition, and action for our people?

Shall not the possession of wealth bring not merely luxury, culture and refinement, but also a high spirit of beneficence guided by justice, and justice adorned with the garlands of benevolence?

Shall we not encourage mankind to higher ends by advancing to public power only the wise, the honorable, and the true, and turning with disdain from the time-servers, demagogues, and plutocrats of our time, who sneer at disinterested efforts and honest attempts to purify and reform our civil service, and believe the best route to success is a "star route?"

Shall we not multiply our charities, and lift from the
weak and unfortunate of our species

> "Their portion of that weight of care
> That crushes into dumb despair,
> One-half the human race!"

If we are to have wealth in houses, lands, in physical
luxuries and comforts, if "palaces are to rise like exhala-
tions, and equipages flash like meteors," let us also create
and foster a wealth of honorable traditions, of lives and
names made glorious and immortal by justice, heroism,
and unselfishness; wealth of art, scholarship, and learning;
wealth of science and philosophy; wealth of public morality,
of charity and religious faith. The strength of a people is
not merely the physical strength, natural advantages, and
material resources. Strong fortresses, chains of mountains,
rugged frontiers and deep seas do not of themselves protect
a country. It is the living wall of brave hearts and willing
arms that constitute its sure and chief defense. The strongest fortress in the known world is the rock of Gibraltar, and
for nearly two centuries it has been held by the mailed hand
of an alien and a stranger; a menace and an abiding reproach to the kingdom and the people who surround it, because a braver and a bolder hand than its natural owners has
taken and withheld it from them.

The essential integer of our country, the seminal principle of American government, the germ of our greatness as
a people, is the independent, fearless, individual man, the
founder and head of the family, whose social and political
influence enlarges itself from the family into the State. For
the family is the birthplace and nursery of the fireside virtues. Home bred—bred at home. Honor, truthfulness
and courage, self-denial and modesty, charity and honesty—
these are the qualities which enlarge their influences from
the home to the neighborhood, until they permeate the community, pervade the State, and public sentiment at last be-

comes imbued with the spirit of personal worth and integrity.

In the ultimate settlement of the gravest affairs of nations, these are the qualities upon which men must rely for safety and good order, and under the form of government we have adopted the need for their cultivation and ascendency seems greater even than elsewhere. They must be represented somewhere in our government. Therefore, whether you call it local self-government or home-rule (which to me has a sweeter sound), I am deeply impressed with the necessity for its restoration in full force in the broad Union, equally for the strength and safety of the Union as well as of these pillars of State, of which that Union is composed, and upon whose integrity it depends; and this is one of the most important duties of the political party to which we are attached.

A proper regulation of the two opposing forces, the centrifugal and the centripetal, maintains a true equilibrium, but for the last twenty years the latter force has been over-exercised, and the former weakened by disuse.

Centralization of power and action is the obvious result of the invention of steam and telegraphy, and the safety of our popular institutions demands decentralization—distribution of power, and its exercise for local self-government by those whose daily lives and interests are to be affected by it. Home-rule, or local self-government, is the right as it is a necessity for the American citizen—and it is the intent and meaning of our written constitution of union.

The strength of a State rests upon the number of upright, independent, self-reliant, self-respecting individuals it contains; and under our democratic theories of government all invasions of individual freedom of conscience and action, not essential for the preservation of social order, and the protection of individual and public rights, are unwise and unwarranted.

All tendencies of legislation which, ignoring individual

responsibility, substitute governmental control in matters social and personal, weakens the powers of the individual, and enfeebling them by disuse, lessens their agency in the good government of himself and his family. In this mischievous substitution of governmental power in matters social and personal lies the objection to sumptuary laws, interference with conscience in social and religious affairs, invasion of the domain of private opinion and personal liberty, which seeks to impose penalties for anticipated acts and offences as yet uncommitted.

This spirit of unwise and unjust interference by the government is the objection to laws which, under the name of taxation, favor certain classes of occupation at the cost of the others, and abridge that freedom of contract and commercial intercourse which an enlightened and enlarged sense of self-interest should control.

It is, in fact, the principle of socialism, of communism, of paternal oversight of the government substituted for individual endeavor, guided by intelligent self-interest, and restrained by individual conscience.

It is to promote the healthy sentiment and habit of self-reliant manhood that the Democratic party throughout the United States insist upon the fullest degrees of individual liberty of conscience and action consistent with public safety and the rights of others; and for that reason we deprecate all unnecessary interference with the rights of local self-government, and all class legislation by the general government which assumes guardianship and protection over the business of the private citizen, and functions of control over matters of domestic and local interest.

We must carefully and jealously insist that the true germ and real basis of the greatness of our country should not be obscured and overlooked, and public control allowed over matters properly belonging to private jurisdiction. We need this as a check upon the centralizing influences, the consolidation of wealth and power, and the tyranny of party organization; all of which tend to wither individual manhood and conscience, and absolve men from the sense of personal duty and obligation.

The emphasis and reiteration of this thought may assist us to comprehend the strength and glory of our free institutions, and the conditions upon which they may secure their perpetuity, and which, if accepted, fastens upon each one of us as an integer in that strength and greatness a fuller sense of his responsibility.

Such contemplation cannot fail to send us back to our respective scenes of labor elevated and invigorated by a comprehension of the trust committed to our hands, so that the political party we sustain shall indeed become worthy means to a noble end, the advancement of the honor and welfare of our country.

Therefore, let us join in the sentiment, "Our Country," May the administration of its government be intrusted only to those who love each member of the Union, and respect equally the rights of each and the rights of all. And may we ever comprehend that our country's greatness consists, not in the wealth of its inhabitants, nor the extent of its dominion, but in the fitness of its people to maintain justice. liberty, and conscientious manhood through the agency of popular self-government.

"DEMOCRACY; PAST, PRESENT AND FUTURE."

Response by Col. William F. Vilas, of Wisconsin, at a banquet of the Iroquois Club, at Chicago, April 13, 1883.

Mr. President, and Gentlemen of the Iroquois Club:

You propose a sentiment as grateful to feeling as it is honorable to discuss in this splendid presence at your festal board. The pure origin, high principles and happy career of the Constitutional Democracy of the Union, as established and conducted by the fathers, are both delightful to contemplate and pregnant with admonition of present duty.

To a lover of his country and his kind, the theme is entrancing, and moderation with difficulty subdues ardor, to make the retrospect a calm lesson.

The success of our Revolutionary arms bestowed on mankind a continent to which princes were strangers, and where the divinity of kingship was laughed to scorn by nature's majesty. The dream of liberty, which for centuries of despotism had tortured humanity like a nightmare, was a waking reality of joy. At last force and law were at one, and the power of government was with the right of government, in the hands of the people to be governed. Happier still, virtue and capability prevailed to sway that scepter. Cromwell could not destroy the king and overturn the kingdom; the blood of his zealots fertilized flowers for Charles the Second, and the commons of Britain remain the empire's third estate to-day. In fortunate America, the opportunity gained by arms was not lost in dissension or smothered by habits.

Wisdom and liberty crystallized in the Constitution, that most blessed work conceived of heaven in the human brain.

Then the great experiment began. A happy flush of enthusiasm and affectionate devotion to the god-like Washington appointed, without division, the opening administration. It was fraternity too pure to long sustain the assault of human passions. America is not Utopia, and divisions must follow inevitable differences. A few years distinguished parties by a line to be expected from human nature and the history of men. It holds to-day, as then, marking the aristocratic greed for special privileges to classes, against the democratic love of common humanity, demanding equal privileges for all. On the one hand gathered they who—though patriotic and manly in resisting the arrogant tyranny of England—yet timidly distrusted the people, favored a strong centralized government, and, under the form of a republic, would have preserved much of the reality of the empire. On the other were the intrepid philosophers and statesmen who accepted the convictions of their logic, religiously loved their race, believed and trusted in the people and regarded all institutions of government only valuable as they subserved the common welfare of equal humanity.

To them, the new Constitution and the new Union were not to establish governors upon and over the people, but a beneficent means by which self-government and individual liberty were forever secured, and the agencies of the popular will defined and limited.

Not in any spirit of demagoguery, nor from any effeminate sentimentalism, but with exalted philanthropy and profound philosophy, and in the strength of freedom, they arrayed themselves as the popular party, and the champions of popular rights. With dramatic fitness, its character was marked, its perpetuity guaranteed, when its foremost banner was flung to the breeze by the hand that penned the declaration of our independence as a Nation, the immortal philosopher and statesman of Monticello, whose fortunate gift to a favored land we choose to celebrate to-night.

Looking over the gulf of war upon the vista of the past, how bright appears the career then inaugurated! From the Presidency of Thomas Jefferson, for half a century and more, with but brief gusts of fitfulness which testified their freedom, the American people confided to that party the keeping of their republic. With the gigantic ease of Atlas, it bore the new world upon its shoulders. In its hands, government was simple, cheap and without burden, and this nation rose before mankind from weakness to power, from poverty to riches, from insignificance to grandeur. By its guidance, the republic obtained, in veritable fact, "her equal station among the powers of the earth," extended her domain to the continent's utmost shore, with her sails whitened every sea, and spread her starry flag, emblem of power, in the skies of every port in the world. Under its care her people advanced in education and intelligence, generally diffused, in riches, well distributed; works of improvement proceeded without overshadowing corporations or depletion of the Nation's treasury, and equality in liberty kept pace with progress in science, arts and material prosperity. Mingling enterprising spirits from every civilized land, our people reveled in the successful "pursuit of happiness," joyous as the laughter of children gathering the fruits of autumn.

Unexpectedly, a fearful tornado fell from this sunny sky, and in its spinning vortex the laws of our liberty and happiness helplessly whirled into chaos, and, finally, lay scattered upon its track, amid the ruins of property and the wreck of ife. And there, in great part, they have been suffered to lie, as if destroyed or valueless, while, with vengeful wrath, the wake of ruin has been cleared. Hate and passion have outvoted every other sentiment, and demagogues have quickly pressed the bellows when the embers cooled. Profiting by the opportunity, conspiracy, in various shapes, has aimed its secret machinations at the dearest privileges of a free people. For party ends, it has strangled the popular voice, to put the reins of power in fraudulent hands; it has perverted and abused the Federal agency, to the injury of local and State government. For private gain, it has corrupted legislation for the use of classes and monopolies, to the enormous acquisition by few of the fruits of the labor of the people. It has made our navy a by-word, and denied to our merchant marine the industries of the sea. It has squandered our wealth of land, and drawn the bars of the treasury that jobbery and robbery might plunder it. And, for both objects, with the spoil of the people, it has inoculated the freeman at the polls with corruption, which steals his manhood as the immoderate cup bereaves the brain.

The practice of tyrannical methods, so long indulged, obediently to natural law, has extended to every phase of political action. It has dominated all the usages of the administration party, until men of independent thought are denied the libery of voice within its pale.

For the extinction of slavery and perpetual security to the Union—the gain of war—the cost of life and wealth the republic could well afford to pay. It cannot afford this additional waste of the safeguards of liberty, unless it speedily cease. It threatens not ourselves and our prosperity alone, but our children and the race.

It avails nothing to criminate or recriminate the authorship or causes. It avails nothing to defend or apologize for the action of the so-called Democratic party of twenty years ago, and later. It must be conceded that it has kept some bad company and been visited with its effects. But "sweet are the uses of adversity;" may we have profited by them!

There must be a change, and a great change; a change of sentiment and a change of methods. The controversies and passions begotten of the war are things of the past, useful only in their teachings of errors to avoid. New ideas, new purposes, new issues and new political associations are before us. Mr. President and gentlemen, the change has already begun. To your credit and honor the keynote of that change, most fruitful to our hope, was sounded at your banquet last year, and resounded with cheerful melody in the elections of last fall.

To overthrow the gigantic forms of error and wrong which have intrenched and fortified, almost unobserved, for these twenty years, will require the concerted energy of all the best of every political complexion. There must be political association to unite them, without animosities to prosecute or revenges to gratify; its face set forward to do the mighty work incumbent on the people of to-day. All philosophy and reason teach that its germ must lie with the party in opposition, for the evils are rooted in the party in administration. But its blossom and fruitage will spring from the hearts and minds of the whole people.

Your conference of last year invited recurrence to the teachings of the fathers for light and inspiration on the path ahead. It is the dictate of wisdom. It will revive a party of the people, instant and zealous, to demand and secure their rights and privileges.

The country needs renewal of the faith and doctrine of the old democracy of Jefferson. Now, as then, it is adequate, and nothing less is adequate, to maintain constitutional government and constitutional liberty. Now, as then, it will prove the road to happiness and prosperity.

We want it, to defend against the Nation's most insidious peril, centralization of powers, unnecessary to the common welfare of the Union. We want it to reform our civil service, to restore honesty, capability and fidelity to supremacy as qualifications for office. We want it to give again purity, integrity, simplicity and economy to the administration of government. We want it to suppress the tyranny of "bossism," and open the ways of political service to self-respecting manhood; to put a period to the canting Pecksniffism in office, which so long has openly prated virtue and secretly practiced iniquity, and give us again the plain and sturdy public servants of the olden days, who are what they seem. We want it, to stop the plunder of office-holders by assessments, and to put down that secret treason of distrust which resorts to corruption as better than argument to win the judgment of the people. We want it for its equality and philanthropy, for its broad faith and intrepid confidence in humanity, for its love of justice to all, for its abhorrence of class favoritism in legislation, taxation and administration.

There rest the principles which must animate and sustain the people's cause in the tremendous conflict immediately impending. I need hardly name it. No man can longer shut his eyes to the open fact. There must and will be aggressive and relentless war against the dominion of monopoly, and the oppression of iniquitous taxation and unjust laws. Many forms of this tyranny beset us. But one overshadows all the rest, demands the earliest redress, and challenges the greatest effort. Its long, felonious tentacles have bound their prehensile grip upon every mode of primary production, every source of wealth. They are fastened upon all parties, all classes and conditions. It is a conspiracy against the people so comprehensive that every community holds its agents, so potential that Congress has obeyed it for more than twenty years. There stands the enemy, there lies the battle-field, and there the battle is at hand! I give you joy in the prospect of it! The foe is sturdy and defiant. From their rampart of riches, piled in menacing mass, the lords of the tariff proclaim their purpose and power to maintain that sum of financial villainy, protective taxation. With skillful ingenuity they have lightened other burdens to make this more secure, and they fill the air with sophistries. The simple question is: Is it right or is it wrong? For, if wrong, it robs the industrious, wealth-producing workers of this country of more than $50,000,000 of their earnings every year to fill the chests of a favored class. If wrong, it is a stupendous wrong. All the doctrines and traditions of democracy, springing from the toil of liberty, cry out against it. It is heresy, false and pernicious, that our millions must labor in forest and field, in counting-room and office, to maintain any class of manufacturers, under pretense of pampering any form of industry. The spoil enriches only the few masters, enervates labor, and strikes enterprise with paralysis. With every material native to our soil, our manufacturers, with profitable adventure, ought to fill our own ships, manned by our own hardy seamen, with products for every buying country on the globe. But what do we see? Our exports are mostly from the farm and mine, carried in the ships of free-trade England; our manufacturing industries fitted and limited only to our fictitious market, with prices upheld by force of legislation, are in a state of intermittent fever, now stimulated to over-production, then gasping with stagnation; while the excellent avocations of ship-building and navigation, which ought to furnish manly industry to hundreds of thousands, languish in decay.

The tariff is a form of slavery not less hateful because the whip is not exposed. No free people can, or will, bear it. There is but one course. The plan of protective robbery must be utterly eradicated from every law for taxation. With unflinching steadfastness, but moderately, without destructive haste or violence, the firm demand of freedom must be persistently pressed until every dollar levied in the name of government goes to the treasury, and the vast millions now extorted for a class are left in the pockets of the people who earn the money. Resolute to defend the sacred rights of property, we must be resolute to redress the flagrant wrongs of property. God forbid that the rights and liberties of this people be laid at the feet of Mammon!

It matters not that this controversy shall divide present houses or break the bonds of past association. Such distresses must not be set in contrast with the welfare of a great nation; they must not stay the demand for justice of a mighty people. Nay, they cannot. Nor any curbs be long applied. They only bind up wrath to burst in greater violence in a day of wrath. There is fearful menace to peace and happiness in the spectacle of injustice with its foot upon the necks of men. Who can fix his contemplation on the glistening splendors of our future without a pang, lest our responsibilities undischarged shall sprinkle the robes of liberty with blood or hamper her limbs with chains?

But I may not weary you with prolonged discussion.

Plant the old standard of constitutional democracy, and beat the long roll! Summon the hosts of liberty, and set your ranks in order! If any fear the battle, send him to the rear! If any will not serve God, but prefer Mammon, give him safe conduct to the enemy! Invoke in the house of counsel the faith and philanthropy of Jefferson; bring again to the field the daring alacrity of Jackson!

And in the sunlight of our Nation's destiny, go "where democratic principles lead the way," to fight the people's enemies and win the people's victories!

"MANIFEST DESTINY."

Response by Col. W. C. P. Breckenridge, of Kentucky, at a banquet of the Iroquois Club, at Chicago, April 13, 1883.

Mr. Chairman and Gentlemen:

We celebrate the natal day of one who was neither soldier, orator, poet, artist nor divine. No sect is called by his name; no graves or bloodstains to sanctify his triumphs; no listening crowds were driven into acts of heroism by the wondrous power of his speech; no songs of his cheer the cottage of the humble, or illuminate the closet of the cultured; nor did his genius add picture, or bust, or monumental pile to the treasures of mankind. Yet he wears a deathless name. In the presence of orators whose eloquence was never surpassed, by the very side of the matchless Patrick Henry, the freeman of orators and the orator of freemen, this silent man stands conspicuous. In an era which gave Washington to freedom and Bonaparte to glory, this swordless man achieved immortality. For a hundred years the songs of the free have been sweeter and happier because of him, and at the symposium of the gifted he would sit an equal and honored guest; all who love religious liberty do just honor to this prophet of universal toleration, and keep fresh his unfading memory with the sweet charity of an unceasing gratitude.

To another has been assigned the grateful task of doing honor to this silent, swordless Thomas Jefferson; to me, the humbler one of giving emphasis to one reason of his

success and of his immortality; one proof of his prophetic
genius and superb gifts. He, more than any man of his
day, foresaw the manifest destiny of his country; and he
more than any other one so shaped the policy of the country
as to realize that destiny.

Would that it were possible for us to enter that plain
frontier home by the babbling Rivana, under the shadow of
the beautiful Blue Ridge, clothed in the palpitating verdure
of a new life—on the spring day 140 years ago—when a
pioneer mother, having passed through the august martyrdom of maternity, lifted up her heart in unutterable thanks-
giving, saying, "I have gotten a man from the Lord," and
putting our ear on her heart catch her musings for the future
of "this man from the Lord." For many centuries every
Jewish mother hoped that her boy might be the Messiah
that was to come. In every age, every mother, knowing
the possibilities of this mysterious and exalted manhood,
sees visions and dreams of her son's future. During the
long watches of that spring night, could it be that a divine
hand drew aside the curtain of the future and gave to this
Virginia mother some glimpses of these full and teeming
days? In her dreams did she see the intervening scenes
from then till now? Did these long years of fruitful glory
and miraculous growth unroll themselves in ever-increasing
radiance? Could we stand at that cradle-side with a clear
and proper apprehension of the world and America as it
then was, and turn our gaze "adown the corridors of time,"
and see the world and America of to-day, we would realize
what the manifest destiny of America then and now means,
and how inextinguishable is the debt mankind owes to him
who lay unconscious in that homely cradle under that low-
eaved roof.

This was before that "Cornet of Horse" found Clive for
India, and Amherst and Wolfe for America; before Wolfe,
on the heights of Abraham, gave his life to conquer this

continent to Anglo-Saxon language, civilization and religion. Less than a million of people scattered along the thin
fringe of the Atlantic had found homes in this new world,
and acknowledged allegiance to the King of Great Britain.
The French and Spanish seemed as likely to dominate over
this Western Hemisphere as the British. Feeble, scattered,
poor—the grain of mustard-seed was not smaller, the little
leaven not more insignificant than these colonies.

Now reverse the picture. Open your eyes in the effulgence of this glorious day, and feast your heart on the picture of this imperial Republic, with its thirty-eight sovereign
States and its growing Territories. Listen to the melodious
hum of its vast industries, the sweet music of its happy and
virtuous homes, the swelling diapason of its perpetual song
of plenty and power; catch the commingling notes from the
turbulent waves of the restless Atlantic, from the placid billows of the murmuring Pacific, and the swash of the great
lakes; hear the intertwining melody of the mighty rivers that
run from friendly lands through united States to protecting
oceans. See the rising smoke—the incense of profitable
labor to a favoring sky curling over crowded cities, prosperous towns and smiling hamlets. Widen the horizon of
your view, and embrace in its broad scope all the English-
speaking peoples of to-day. Compare our republic and
these peoples with the rivals of 1743—the French and the
Spaniard. This is what no one foresaw on that spring day
in 1743, but this is what Jefferson did afterward foresee and
labored to produce.

More than any man in his day he foresaw the future and
what was necessary to accomplish this result. To his far-
seeing prescience the destiny was clear—to his equal statesmanship the means were also clear. And so great was he
that what we see was not the end he foresaw; we are yet
but at the threshold of the beginning; we are yet but at

the base of the mighty fabric whose corner-stone he helped to lay. Like him and his compeers, we are only builders.

The principles by whose subtle and pervasive power these mighty changes have been wrought were not the creation of Jefferson; they were inwrought into our nature as men. But he apprehended them with absolute clearness; he loved them with ardent devotion; he trusted in them with implicit faith; he gave his life to make them regnant. All the circumstances, physical, mental and moral, surrounding that generation were divinely favorable, even though apparently so adverse. The new country, the separating oceans, the diverse colonies, the absence of all neighbors, rendered such an experiment made by such people on such principles easy of success. But they were wise and great men who could for such principles make such sacrifices, and for such an end adopt such means. These principles they classified as universal, founded in the nature of man as man; as historic, settled by the bloody contests of all the past; as governmental, applying to the peculiar situation of themselves and their posterity. The fundamental principles of universal application found their Jeffersonian form in the preamble and first paragraph of the Declaration of Independence, in words we cannot repeat too often nor meditate on too much. These principles are founded on the laws of nature and nature's God, they find their root in the brotherhood of man and the Fatherhood of God, and from this root spring all that has made this wondrous growth possible. All men are created equal, and are endowed by their Creator with inalienable rights. This is the basis of all political truth. The next step is that "to secure these rights governments are instituted among men;" but these governments derive their just powers from the consent of the governed. This is the basis of all governmental forms and policy. Freemen, created by God, with inalienable rights, instituting a government to secure these rights, and basing all its powers on their consent, was the only conception of a true government that our fathers had. But to these universal truths were added the historic rights which our fathers had inherited as Englishmen, or been granted as American colonists. These gave Parliamentary representation, laws enacted in an orderly method by representatives of the people properly chosen—the indissoluble connection between taxation and representation, liberty of person, security of property, voice in the government.

Jefferson saw clearer, if not sooner than his compeers, that new life and greater scope must be given to these principles. He was in its loftiest sense a Democrat; he loved, he trusted the people; he loved his race; he was indeed a man, and there was nothing human that was foreign to him. He deified man as man, and despised and feared all that could create classes or ranks. Man as man was free and capable of self-government—was the postulate of all his thinking. This was the starting point of all his meditations. All men ought to be free, all men shall be free, all men will be free was the conviction, the resolve, the hope of his life. His part was to assist in making America free. This was duplex—one part was to secure such a government as would protect and maintain freedom; the other was to establish a policy that would in the end embrace the continent. This was a sublime conception, wrought out in its mighty details with a wisdom, a courage, a patience never surpassed, and by successive generations of men, who have builded perhaps wiser than they knew. The form of government actually adopted was not precisely in all its details what he preferred, but the pervasive power residing in its principles was such that, with his guidance, it wrought the desired result. It became, it is, it will remain, if his disciples are put in power, "an indissoluble union of indestructible States," a republic of sovereign States, one as to all the world and all federal concern; but as to all State matters, jealously many; each in its sphere, and to the extent of its powers, sovereign and independent. The constitution, and not the discretion of those in power is at once the warrant and the measure of the powers to be exercised; there residing nowhere any power, except as therein granted. With such a government, expansion was possible; neither the number nor the size of the States, nor the extent of population or territory, need cause alarm or change. Logically—philosophically, a hundred sovereign States with full populations could be united under such a constitution, based on such underlying principles. Whenever their joint power was sufficient to protect from external danger, there was no necessary limit to expansion. And with such principles separation, if it ever came, might be only temporary. If men are free—if governments are founded on the consent of the governed; if local governments are sovereign, and federal governments can be limited by written compacts or constitutions, then the possibility of expansion and modification of mere forms becomes infinite. If the object of all governments is to protect these inalienable rights, and freemen can secure that protection by a union of States under one compact, then there is no permanent failure of free government possible except on the single hypothesis that man is incapable of self-government.

Jefferson rejected this hypothesis for himself, his race and his country, accepted with a loving, trusting faith in mankind the verity of his hopes. But there must be room for development of such principles, and he held the continent to be ours. This was the cherished hope of many of that day. Neither mountain nor river, nor savage, nor Frenchman, nor Spaniard, nor wilderness was permitted to obstruct this glorious view of a homogeneous and ocean-bound republic of freemen. They were pioneers of a new and magnificent world. The ancient kingdoms were to be surpassed by this new people for whom God had preserved this virgin and enchanting continent. The frozen North and the tropic South were to prosper under one flag—the flag of the free. This new empire was to dictate law to the world, restore peace to the earth, give liberty to the oppressed. Here were ample homes to be found for the poor and plenty for the starveling. The new era of a nobler brotherhood, the sunlit dawn of a new day had begun, and mankind was to find ampler room and fresher fields for higher development. To Jefferson these dreams were actualities, and with a minuteness of details and a practical statesmanship that were equal to the prophetic conception, he secured religious freedom by the abolishment of a State religion; he destroyed an aristocracy based on wealth by abolishing the law of entails and primogeniture; he made naturalization easy; he dedicated the Northwest to a common country and to become free States; he ordered George Rogers Clark to seize the bank of the Mississippi River; he aided the pioneers of Kentucky to form a new State on the basis of universal suffrage, and equal representation based on numbers, and tried with almost superhuman powers to abolish slavery. By these wonderful achievements, the new republic began its career with the freedom of religion, freedom from possible aristocracy and the certainty of the addition of new States. But he felt that he wanted no neighbors, and so came about the purchase of Louisiana, which will be held to be an achievement in wisdom and statesmanship only surpassed by the Declaration of Independence. It gave us more than that magnificent territory—it settled our national policy. He said: "Objections are raising to the eastward against the vast extent of our boundaries, and propositions are made to exchange Louisiana or a part of it for the Floridas. But as I have said, we will get the Floridas without," and this settled policy was to carve new States out of this far-reaching territory, or, as he put it, "when we shall be full on this side we may lay off a range of States on the western bank from the head to the mouth, and so range after range, advancing as we multiply," and under this policy we have acquired the Floridas and Texas, and to the Pacific shore.

Have we reached the end? Has the future no conquests for freedom? Must we live in the past, and content ourselves with recounting the triumphs of the fathers? Shall our sons have no laurels of their own winning to wear? When another hundred and forty years have passed away, and in some great city which, like this, has sprung up as if by magic into power and wealth, in some noble hall, amid another assemblage of notables, of what will that American who responds to another similar toast have to boast? What can limit the horizon of our hopes? What may we not expect? As we recall all the glories of the past, as we exult in the prosperity of the present, why should we doubt the possibilities of the future? It has in store its own conquests—conquests by steam and commerce and inevitable fate.

My brethren, I have heard much of a revival of the faith of our fathers, of going back to the days of the fathers. I pray for the spirit of the fathers. Democrats, our fathers were progressive; they believed in the people, they trusted the people, they were the true radicals. We must raise once more the standard of the Democracy that was once full of hope, candor and courage, for it had no secrets, it had no improper object, and it had the people at its back. I pray for the revival of that courage—a courage that shot deserters, and made no compromise of principle for expediency; for a revival of that candor that kept nothing hid because it felt that there was nothing of which it needed to be ashamed. It was a simple creed our fathers held, a federal government supreme in its sphere of limited and delegated powers; State governments sovereign in their sphere; an impartial and just distribution of the public burdens, so imposed that each paid his share, and only his share, of the public tax; no imposition of taxes for any purpose other than a public and governmental object; a strict economy in the public service; a rigorous responsibility in the expenditure of the public moneys; a sound currency based on coin; careful regard for all contracts, and scrupulous performance thereof according to their tenor; implicit obedience to the law; absolute protection at home and abroad of every American citizen; the freedom of person, of speech, and of franchise; the purity of the elective franchise, and prompt obedience to the will of the people as expressed at the polls; cordial relations with all the world on the recognized condition that no foreign power should have a new foothold on this continent; warm sympathy for all people not so free as we; an earnest welcome to all who would cast their lot with us; absolute faith in the honesty, courage and intelligence of the people, and in the growth, wisdom and prosperity of their country. Let this be our creed to-day, and we will achieve for our posterity what the fathers did for us. Our destiny is certain. We may be the leaders in the events which will mark our history, or others may lead us. To lead we must have the confidence of the people, and must deserve that confidence. Whenever they believe that the Democratic party do believe in that creed, and will in good faith administer the government in the spirit of Jefferson and Jackson—in the spirit of economy and progress, of courage and fidelity— we will be given power. The people know their power, and our country's destiny. They will follow where men lead. There is no antagonism between the sections. Justice to each and all is possible, and I plead to-night for a renewal of that spirit which knew the interests and rights of each State and section and gave to all equal protection. Inscribe on our banners to-night equal and exact justice

to every citizen and every State; a just distribution of the public burden; faithful fulfillment of every obligation; strict economy in the public service; trust in the future—one flag, one country, one destiny—and we can repeat, in the hopeful words of him whose natal day we celebrate: "We should have such an empire for liberty as she has never surveyed since this creation; and I am persuaded no constitution was ever before so well calculated as ours for extensive empire and self-government."

"THE GREAT NORTHWEST."

Response by Gen. J. C. Black, of Illinois, at a banquet of the Iroquois Club, at Chicago, April 13, 1883.

Mr. Chairman: In his absence you have requested me to bend the bow of Ulysses, and if I prove unequal to the task, you will have to remember it is because you have this evening violated established Democratic principles of equality, and placed me, without warning, in the company of acute critics, to follow and to be followed by splendid orators of silver tongues and melodious speech, whose every word has had the deliberation of thought, the polish of premeditation and the fire of ambition, and who nobly have spoken before you for the establishment and maintenance of great Democratic doctrines. I have had no time for this theme to-night, because I havs listened with charmed senses to the splendid oratory which has poured upon us.

I would have been more than mortal if the eloquent voices of the Northwest had not won me from all selfish considerations to listen while they spoke the immortal truths upon which the great Democratic party at one time held, and will again possess the political allegiance of the great Northwest.

The theme itself must furnish me inspiration, or I must fail; and when I think of the fact that it has been scarcely a hundred years since the moccasined foot of the pioneer broke the long silence of this region which geologists tell us is the oldest, and which history shows has been reserved by fortune for liberty; when I think of that short recorded career, and then see around me the glorious physical, material, and moral results, I stand surprised, impressed, with the majesty of the subject. (Applause.) It has not been a hundred years since the war-whoop of the original Iroquois died away, and to-night their gentle and civilized echoes sound from the center of the great metropolis of the Northwest, whose ten thousand furnaces burn where the wigwam's solitary embers were. (Applause.)

This day, to-night, and in the presence of this assembly, is a fitting time for retrospection as well as for prophecy. For he whose anniversary this is, was the man who, by his diplomacy, won the broad west from foreign control, and by his statesmanship dedicated it forever to the highest experiment of mankind. (Applause.) The Northwest is great in many particulars; greatest of all, gentlemen, in this, that while the clank of chains has been heard in every other land, while men have in all other regions been obliged to struggle against the spirit of caste or the power of tradition, this land, from the very first hour in its civilized history, until now, has been dedicated forever to freedom, and Jefferson's was the hand which wrote on its portals that slavery and involuntary servitude, save for crime, should never be tolerated here. (Applause.) Before that, as Col. Breckinridge has told you, the prophetic soul of Jefferson studied this vast area, and assigned here the seat of empire, and sent scouts and pioneers to keep and hold it against all comers. When the expedition of Lewis and Clark wound its way through the Alleghanies and penetrated these forests, and came down and across these broad rivers, and over these mighty prairies, its men were the Democratic pioneers, establishing here his place for the freedom of mankind. From that time until now, with varying fortune the sentiments which Jefferson inculcated, and which he wrote preparatory to the ordinance creating the Territory of the Northwest, and ceding it to the Union, have been prominent in all its enactments; have been established in all of its constitutions; and the result has been all that he ever hoped for. Free men in all sections of the world have turned to this land as the worshiper turned his eyes to the Mecca of his faith. The men who toiled in Europe, or who came from the plains of far-away Asia, or slipped the lash of an ignoble servitude at home or abroad, sought out this region because, of all the republics, it was the land of liberty; because the traditions of the people, as far as their few years could make tradition, were, that every institution of government and of law should be made and maintained solely as it was beneficent to the people; because here was no remotest taint of feudatory wrong; because it was established here in our fundamental law that the people should own their soil. Freedom cannot live in a country where the people do not own the land. A simple truth, and yet the struggles of six thousand years were needed for its establishment. The root of the great tree of liberty must strike down through the possessions of those who are to be its supporters. (Applause.) It must grow upon free land; it must grow upon land that can be aliened, that cannot be transmitted by forced inheritance or entail, that can be moved as any other property can be moved and as freely. (Applause.) Thomas Jefferson, in the house of Burgesses of Virginia, began the long struggle against primogeniture and entail, which had created the grand estates of Europe; and he assisted in establishing that condition of freedom of the soil in all the Northwest which now exists; he did more than that; and the morning of the Northwest was when he and his fellow Virginians handed this territory over to the republic and to humanity, and said, that in addition to the ownership of the soil, the citizens had a greater right, and that was the ownership and control of their own government; and I say, Mr. President, that no people, who own their soil and may freely transfer it and control their constitution and their laws, and every creature under them, need fear despotism or the loss of their liberties, and without these united, the greatest prosperity itself becomes simply the source for a people's oppression. (Applause.)

The pioneers who entered upon and subdued these regions of freedom and of liberty came without the aid of government. They found the pathway of empire open; they occupied it and established their own State systems, making them free to all men as they had found the virgin territory; barring out every phase of oppression as far as they could; determined only that they would leave the country as they had found it, a heritage of liberty.

It is worthy of notice that all the States of the great Northwest were admitted under Democratic administration and were Democratic in their origin. Every constitution of every State, carved from the Territory of the Northwest, was Democratic handiwork; each member thereof became a State under Democratic control and Democratic administration, and they retained their Democratic dominance, and their Democratic principles in the National Government, and in the control of the State institutions, until the fearful passions of civil war swept men from their allegiance.

There was, in addition to these doctrines of individual liberty, of local government and of the right of ownership in the soil, the fourth doctrine inculcated by Jefferson and by the great Democratic party; and that was, that the Union had a right to perpetuate itself, and so when the time came that evil counsel rent a great party, it was found that the evil counselors were not able to carry the party with them, and here in the Northwest, the Democracy (if the great gentlemen who preceded me will allow me to say so), the Democracy of twenty years ago, were, as they are now, faithful to the Federal Union, faithful with purse, with blood, with their sons, with their whole fortunes, and with their lives; and the consequence was, that when the work of the whole people had been done, and the Nation had been re-established and restored, the honor was not to any party alone, but it was to all parties, and to all men in the great Northwest. (Applause.)

Fellow citizens, we stand in the center of an empire; the glorious empire of liberty and law; an empire of which this is the capital, and where is established the oracle of the thought of the Northwest; no voice is more potential in establishing the destinies of this great future-growing people, than the voice of the Democracy, as you have assembled it in annual council at this place.

And when Democracy shall return to power, as it has in four of the five great States, and taken possession again in the State of Illinois and re-established its dominion over the land of its youth and glory, honor will be given to the efforts of this club for the restoration of Democracy to its original place in the hearts of the people of the Great Northwest.

Here, under the teaching of this man Jefferson, of those that he inspired and were his disciples, and over all this territory, the national Democracy established the system of free schools, and endowed them liberally, so that to-day the silver hand of learning opens the door of the common schools to every child of the republic, no odds how poor its parentage or how despised its religion. The great National Democracy established the doctrine that here should be actual, civil and religious liberty, and to-day, as a consequence, the worshiper of any faith may build his shrine, and build it protected by the administration of Democratic law, and traditions of Democratic doctrine, and to-day, whether he be worshiper of Buddha, whether he be a follower of the faith of some Asiatic fanaticism, or whether he worships at the shrine of the pure religion of our time, here is equal protection to all; and in that is found the best development of religious thought. And that has been a part of the heritage which the great Northwest received from this man Jefferson, and has helped to transmit to posterity.

I can think of a great Northwest of which this is but the foundation. Behold the highways and palaces of commerce, the broad fields of agriculture, the deep down wealth of mines. The voices of your orators to-night will sound to-morrow morning from this great center in the ears of fifty million people. The words of wisdom or of folly that you speak will from the heart of this great Northwest be wired to all the hamlets and homes of the land, and it will be asked by men, "How is the great Northwest going in the political struggle that is now impending, and which we are about to enter upon?" Will it go Democratic, or will it follow some ancient hate, and feed fat some bloody grudge and go against Democracy? That depends, gentlemen, how closely the Democratic party shall adhere to the traditions of its Democratic founder, established by him in the greatest document that has ever been prepared by man; a document which I believe with all my heart is the supreme and greatest utterance of uninspired mind; a document which drew into its composition all the experience of mankind; a document which was touched by the hand of genius and animated by the life love of humanity, and which holds in undying characters the great charter of humanity; that one man is created the equal of every other man; that his government and every institution thereof and thereunder endures solely for him and for his uses and prosperity, and is subject to be altered and changed and modified at his will, in order that it may grow with his growth and strengthen with his strength.

The future of the Northwest is something that the dreamer himself may not predict. Where fifteen millions are now, fifty millions will stand, if the doctrines that brought fifteen millions here and that opened the doors of the wilderness are maintained in their purity. Other lands have had their swarming myriads and the only monuments left of them are graven upon the marble, granite or brass; they are buried by sands; they are obliterated by the tooth of time; but the monuments that this people build to-day in their institutions, if they are faithful to their Democratic ancestral doctrines, will endure to the last, firm and immutable.

"TYPICAL MEN."

Response by Rev. Wm. E. Park, at a dinner of the Republican Club of New York, February 15, 1896.

Mr. President, Gentlemen of the Republican Club: As a speaker this evening I feel myself to be under some special disadvantages. I have not the environment which the rest of you have. I have come from the section of the country that may be considered more rural. I do not often have an opportunity to listen to such speakers as you have listened to to-night, and I feel a little bewildered under such intoxicating influences, an influence to which you are accustomed (laughter) ; but to me it is very new. And if in my mind there should be any element of confusion from my situation, let me quote two lines of a poem that I saw in the New York Tribune after a dinner when a man came home in a confused state of mind; his wife accused him of something that he was not guilty of and he replied:

> "You think me with whisky
> My brain is bedewed,
> You mistake me, my dear,
> I am Chauncey Depewed."

And, being a minister, I look out for Scriptural fulfillment. Why, the psalms are getting realistic to me. The last speaker personified those illustrious words of David, "Lo, I come" (laughter), and I feel myself under some embarrassment and have something the sensation of a cat in a strange garret when I, a poor minister, am placed in contact with such statesmen, men whose names go all over the country and whose pictures are seen in every edition of the New York dailies. For there is no mistake about it, a minister is most shamefully misunderstood at times. I knew a pious mother that was explaining to her little girl the condition of the Holy Martyrs thrown to the lions. She was misunderstood. Said the little one: "Ma, that little lion out in the back corner isn't getting nothing." (Laughter.)

And then again a minister is misunderstood most shamefully in his professional labors. I knew a minister at one time who exchanged with one of his clerical brethren, and during the most powerful passages of his eloquence he saw a woman dressed in black who was soaking her handkerchief with her tears. He learned her name and he inquired her residence; he called upon her the next day, desiring to apply the sermon to her mind, but with a sort of secret squint of the eye, hoping that he might get a compliment for his discourse. "I called, madam," said he, "because I saw you were deeply affected during my discourse yesterday afternoon." "I was, I was, very much." "And I called to see if it could not be applied to your condition; and if I could not follow up the sermon by some practical remarks." "You are so kind, sir, I will take you into my confidence. I am a widow woman, as you see by my dress and manner; but I had a cow that I thought the world of; and I spent all my time a-feeding that cow and a-stroking that cow and a-patting that cow and talking to that cow, and it really begins to take the place of my husband (laughter). And the cow's name is Nellie, and day before yesterday I couldn't find Nellie anywhere, and I went to the barn, walked in and she was not there, and I says, 'Where is Nellie?' and I remembered there was a pond and quagmire around the house, and I went there and my worst fears were more than realized, there was Nellie going down and down, and I couldn't see anything but her horns and the line of her back and her tail, and said I, 'Farewell, Nellie, farewell, Nellie,' and she raised her head out of the mud and gave one last bellow of farewell to me, and your voice yesterday afternoon did sound so much like it" (laughter and renewed laughter), and she broke down again and tears began to roll down her cheeks. But now, gentlemen of the club, let us get at business. (Laughter.)

I am to speak on the subject of typical men, and I want to know if you cannot join me in doing a little historic work. It may take a little thought; but what is anything worth without thinking or what conclusion is worth anything which we arrive at without some exertion. I hold that ideas are eternal; but men change, and ideas are beautiful only as they incarnate themselves in men and representative men. The interest of an age is sometimes centered in a single man, like Cicero or Charlemagne, and we behold a planet. Sometimes it incarnates itself in a set of men and we behold a brilliancy or a set of asteroids; sometimes the genius of the age incarnates itself in many divine men moving together, and we behold the luminous galaxy like the Nebulæ, which is the result of the net returns by stars and planets by the thousand. I am to speak of some of the representative men of the ages at critical periods in the history of the world. I suppose that about the middle of the first century the Roman power had incarnated in itself the whole civilized world. Rome was victorious by sea and land, her helmets glittered on every shore, her lances and swords sparkled in every sun then shining on the earth. All opposition to the Roman power had died away from the mind of sensible and practical men, opposition to Rome was only the part of the fool, the crank, the fanatic. The institution of slavery was at that time considered to be reasonable and thoroughly wise. It was the method by which the strong men could oppress the weak, and it was considered to be the best ordinary and established method of making use of the lower orders of society. The whole idea was that the capitalist should own the stock and the labor, and one had no more scruple in dealing in his fellow men commercially than he would in handling goods or any regular product of commerce. The idea of the world was unbroken, but on one day there appeared on the summit of Mars Hill an old man, of bodily presence weak, and of speech contemptible; and Athens, the old historic rock from which the Persians had hurled their missiles, which they expected to result in the enslavement of Greece, and five hundred years before a man stood around the base of Mars Hill, and said those extraordinary words, "That God hath created of one blood all nations of men." Perhaps, being a minister, I think unduly of this passage, but, after some study of history, I am inclined to attribute to it a stupendous political importance. It was the first codified statement of the equality of man, an idea which has been foreshadowed and implied in the teachings of Jesus Christ; but now it was distinctively formulated by the great Apostle. A seed of thought was planted in the mind of the world, a seed of thought that never died, because I shall endeavor to show it was in an American President the fulfillment of the direction of the Apostle found final and practical realization. Twelve centuries roll away. Mighty changes have occurred. The vast and colossal Roman Empire fell, crumbled into fragments. She had been dispelled by the milder—milder but stronger—forces of granite, for the Roman Empire was, after all, of the earth earthy.

It was material, and material things live because the

world cannot get on without them. The pyramids of Egypt
are left to grow old and hoary, and the monuments of Egypt
are as a fossil on the Nile, for men can easily do without
them. They cannot do without moral truth. They cannot
do without the eternal idea. But when the vast Roman
Empire rolled down, shivered into fragments, each fragment became a little kingdom in itself, and Rome broke
into feudalism. Men were too busy with their feuds to see
where the real interest of the world lay, and the wise men
of the time did not turn their eyes to the little colonies in
tne northeast corner of Europe, where were gathering the
influence that would result in another colossal dominion.
Then I claim that it is said that God uses the talents and
ability of men to still greater degree, and it is interesting to
see how the world has been benefited by certain co-ordi-
nations and mutual relations, of the weakness and strength.
The Norman King, Plantagenet Kings from the time of
William the Conqueror, had been men of consummate
ability; the Kings of France had been slothful, imbecile and
cowardly, but one King of France, Philip Augustus, was a
consummately supremely able man, and the Roman
Pontiff, Innocent III., was at that time the most capable
and the most determined man among public characters then
living. It occurred to the Barons of England, who for some
time had been getting and growing stronger, that with some
assistance from the Roman See they might be able to wring
from that wretched King John, who was a vile old imbecile
and dastardly coward, some concessions of his very dearest
privileges. They assembled their vassals and they met him
upon the plain of Runnymede. It was, and must have been
a scene romantic beyond description as the Barons moved
to and fro, their helmets and chain mail glistening in the
sun, their plumes waving. The great charter was prepared
—a great charter which, in my opinion, had the germs of
the liberation of England; ultimately of America and the

whole Anglo-Saxon race. It was provided there that the villeins, or the serfs, and half the people of England were then serfs, should never have the cart or the plow attached for a debt. It was provided that no man should be condemned without the judgment of his peers—the beginning of the trial by jury. It was provided that the nobles might come at the call of the King, and tenants at will, it was the embryo House of Lords and House of Commons. In the name of the Barons, Sir Philip Fitzwalter demanded of the wretched King that he sign the instrument. King John hesitated and Sir Philip Fitzwalter very leisurely drew his sword. The great document is signed, the liberties of the Saxon race are secured and England owes more to the weakness of her King at that time than to the transcendent abilities of monarchs who came before and followed after. (Applause.)

Five centuries roll away and mightier yet are the changes. The spirit of enterprise engrafts herself in Columbus. It as about that time that Johann Gutenberg invented the movable type, which gave, as we say, wings and legs to idea.

Soon after that—soon by the historic period there were settlements along the Atlantic seaboard where about thirteen independent States were strung upon a slender level along the eastern seacoast and slowly groping up to the Alleghenies. The colonies had learned by successful repulsion of invasions by the Indians and French, something of their power, and begun to find out something of their own resources; the stupidity of the English Government at this crisis surpassed all belief. The glorious age of Chatham had passed away and Lord North led the King in their feeble councils. With inconceivable folly the British Government, by enacting the Stamp Act, irritated and enraged the colonists and lost a hold on all the hope of future America for the sake of a tax that was not worth $60,000, if it could have been collected. By the duty of 3d. a pound on tea she irritated the colonists by a tax from which she never derived $50 in actual value, and at last by the inconceivable folly of bringing on a little skirmish called the Battle of Lexington, she lost her hold on the continent for the sake of securing thirty-six barrels of gunpowder that she never got, after all. (Laughter.) The typical men of the time appeared in the Continental Congress; and by the exigency of the time suddenly lifted into supreme power, they met to launch a new nation into the world, and in what world did they launch it? Mighty events had been formed and were about to be. Frederick the Great walks with tottering steps in the garden of Sans Souci; he thinks of Luther and Rossbach, the great drill sergeant of Europe; thou shalt next think of the grave. Maria Theresa, all faithful and anxious for the end, walks the gardens of Schonbrunn, in Prussia; Catherine II. is passing away amid the glitter of her own ice palaces in Moscow. There is a strong man that appears in France, now at Strasburg and now at Metz; his name is Gabriel Honore Riqueti as well as Comte de Mirabeau. He is obscure and low-lived, but he will shake thrones. The great apostle of skepticism had just died, the Marquis de Voltaire. He aimed to attack superstition, but before he was through he waged war on faith itself. There were existing then two remarkable boys, one upon the Island of Corsica, and another one, Arthur Wellesley, in the strife in Egypt. The one would be like the volcano sending its bolts up into heaven, and the other was fated to be the gravity that drew them down. And in America mighty changes were beginning, and the Continental Congress, early in June, began to adopt the subject of separation. The final moment was reached, and at last, although the guiding mind of the movement, George Washington, was encamped by the City Hall Park, in this city, very near to where we now are, the assembly was had through the mind of Thomas Jefferson, with assistance from Adams and from Franklin, who acted through the hand of John Hancock. There was deliberation in that great moment when a nation came into life, and with the message the usher of the Congress said to the boy in waiting: "Tell the man to ring," and the man in the belfry shook the old bell upon which were engraved the words "Proclaim liberty to all the inhabitants thereof." The new nation was born and a new hemisphere was detached from the old conservatism of Europe, and the history, and the future of the world, leaving the past to the old world, the future of the world and that of mankind was in the hand of the United States forevermore. (Great applause.)

I shall say what I think. What else can I say? I do not know but that our fathers have been in some respects overpraised. They liberated the continent, but imperfectly. It was not all done. It is something grotesque to see that they never noticed the inconsistency of freeing one race and allowing that race to enslave another. Now, the logic of the situation is that if you tie a chain around the neck of the slave you tie the slave to you, but you are attached to him and the other end of the chain is around the master's neck also.

Gentlemen, it is a peculiarity of work in this world that imperfect effort, or whatever may be accomplished by it, always leaves the imperfection as the most active and prominent feature. You have a shoe made of the finest materials, but there is one interfering peg or nail; all your attention is fixed upon the defective part. (Laughter.) You do not notice the merits of the rest. It was just so with the American Constitution that trouble came from the imperfect work. Just as the trouble of the Israelites, when they reached the promised land there came the Hittites and Philistines, whom they failed to subdue at the proper time. It is singular to see how rapidly and how thoroughly slavery displaced all other political questions and placed itself before the world and the country as the one living issue. I do not know but that the next generation feared the inevitable war a little too much. Perhaps they were timid in trying to postpone doing, but it was very natural. There was a whole aye of compromise, but Clay, Webster and Thomas Benton never did fairly convince the world that that which was morally wrong could be politically right. An obscure man then declared before the Illinois Legislature that the Union could not exist half slave and half free, and the prophecy of Cassandra was for the time being unnoticed. Wise men began to see that the country could be settled only by the bloodiest war, but where is the pilot who can guide the ship through the coming storm, and who is the one that will lead us in the gigantic contest? Far away on the prairies of the West the man was preparing, and when the tale of bricks is accomplished there was a master who had been trained and was ready to come. The spirit of a coming which had incarnated itself some years before in a typical man, who was born about as far from great things as any one well could be. I do not know a character in history that shows so great a difference between his early promise and the immense subsequent result. The genius of civilization passed by the men of the schools, the learned, the high and the mighty, and she incarnated herself in a railsplitter, a raftsman on a flatboat, an unsuccessful merchant and dealer in stories, rather more pointed than refined, and a man who began life as a laborer, and finally as a lawyer, found perhaps from the working of his own conscience and moral nature very limited success at the beginning of his profession. But I hold, Mr. President, the peculiar and matchless spirit of Lincoln over all the men of his time was in his capacity for measureless growth. There was in him the indefinable, subtle and literally limitless expansion. He resembled the Afreet in the Arabian story, chained down and penned into the bottle of smoke; you would look first and say, why a little can hold the whole of him, but the smoke ascended to the heavens and lo! we have the Afreet whose feet are on the earth and whose head seems to brush the very stars of heaven.

The vast expansion of Lincoln's character came from his extraordinary moral character and his extraordinary intellectual nature. I say his extraordinary moral nature. For it is an idea of mine, and I believe it is true, that the moral faculties can be just as much a seat of genius as the intellectual. There was in Lincoln an honesty, a candor of nature, a love of the right, a certain reality, a sense of the real, that made him the best adapted of any man of his time to burst the bubble, to shake down the shame, to come to real point and essence of the fact. There was not one in his time that excelled him in a certain ability to take all the complications of a situation, throw some conditions away as so much mere chaff and stand and put his finger directly on the hinging point. With this there was a marvelous power of what I call clear, explicit statement; a wonderful skill in the writing, plotting, and arranging of his ideas; an ability to put things before other minds in a way to carry his point so that while he appeared to feel he was invisible, and unconsciously the leader, and left men to follow him under the pleasing delusion that they were only carrying out their own minds (applause) ; he had drawn his resources from others, but more from himself. Surrounded by the coarse companionship, the eye of genius could see objects invisible to other minds; he enriched his mind from the half dozen books that he could get, and it was a mercy to him that he only had half a dozen, for he was able to master them. He was trained in ways that he knew not for his great position, and, as in the case of the Barons and King John, the very deficiencies of Lincoln were favorable to his success. Gentlemen, very often men owe success to a mere deficiency. It was that that made the military strength of Grant and the Duke of Wellington that they had almost no imagination, and they were never deceived by fears or mistakes in the future. Lincoln's want of conventional refinement brought him nearer to the heart and made him more popular with the masses, and there was a kind of slowness in the workings of his mind, because he was a Caesar, that had to take the people constantly into partnership. It was not possible, as we see now, to get the victory too soon, he had to wait until the people came to his way of thinking. He was moving on to destinies of which he suspected nothing. There was no one that ever saw where he would ultimately be. He was an enigma to those around him, for he spoke the last word of the new movement and no one could yet read it. He was obliged to incorporate himself with the great political revolution until he fairly obliged the revolution to incorporate itself in him. (Applause.)

The key of the situation was in the hand of this remarkable man, though he did not know it. A succession of astonishing events, combinations of his own ability and the vital force of circumstances, wafted him into the place of power. From the standpoint of national observation he discovered what had undoubtedly been undiscovered for a long time before, that all the troubles, delays and difficulties of the country centered in slavery, and he made up his mind that slavery must go. He was not assisted much. He treaded the winepress alone. There is something more than in one self-contented man thinking out himself the whole problem of the country and curing the disease of the age. He was strong and he was yielding. He had not strength like a stone buttress, but rather that of the wire cable. On the 21st of September, 1862, he met his cabinet, and, as has been said, he read them a page or two of

Artemus Ward; it was one of the grandest efforts in the history of the world—the meeting of that cabinet was on a par with the Declaration of Independence or the meeting of the Barons at Runnymede; and then he showed them a draft of a proclamation, to be adopted without debate as to its essential points, that slaves were to be made free on an appointed day. At the suggestion of Secretary Seward he waited, and wisely, until he could connect his mighty movement with some sort of a victory. The Battle of Antietam occurred as a fact; the proclamation was made known upon the 22d day of September, and it went into effect in January of the following year. I do not know whether history ever shows a movement that was more thoroughly wise or more consummately adroit; it exposed the rebels' position completely; it put them before the world as the avowed defenders of the vilest institution on the face of the earth, and foreign governments who would try to assist them must pose themselves before the world as defenders of slavery alone. Moral victory. A new heart in the nation, sprung from the national endorsement of the right side; the strong army of Ulysses Grant was the hand that carried out the magnificent Lincoln thought. Glorious nation! Victories followed in succession, Vicksburg was broken down and the Mississippi swept unretarded to the sea; and on the 1st of January, 1863, or as soon after as war could effectuate it, slavery disappeared from the United States, a few years after it disappeared from the whole civilized world, and the fulfillment of the Apostle Paul's prophecy, "God hath created in one blood all nations of men," found its realization in that tremendous thought of the railsplitter of Illinois. (Great applause.)

That was the beginning and end of the slavery question. Gentlemen of the Republican Club, we may approach another; we think too much of epochs. They only indicate the last of a succession of steps. The long hand of the clock runs over fifty-nine minutes, it passes another minute, and we count time from another hour; the last minute would have no importance if it were not for the fifty-nine that went before it. The epoch is approaching now; the epoch is eternal. I am interested as a minister in the doctrine of apostolic succession. I do not believe in the succession by the laying on of hands, but I do believe in the transmission of a hero. Ideas are eternal. But men who incarnate the ideas ever change. Gentlemen of the Republican Club, the spirit of the apostle on Mars Hill, the spirit of the Barons of Runnymede, the spirit of the Continental Congress, the spirit of Abraham Lincoln is with you. You are the heirs of it and it is for you to carry it on. It is the glory of a past example that can be adapted to new issues and to changing conditions. It is beneath us, gentlemen, to be guilty of the folly to endeavor to imitate the technical acts of a hero, but we can make his spirit immortal. It would be folly to run into the Red Sea because the Israelites did; the waves might not divide, and we would only get drowned. It would be folly to set apples on little boys' heads and begin shooting at them with bow and arrow because William Tell did. It would be perfect folly to get a hatchet and run around chopping down cherry trees and then go and say, "Father, I can't tell a lie," because George Washington did. That kind of imitation is the imitation of a fool, but the spirit of these heroes can be incarnated in us, and we can go on doing what they would do if they were in our places and in our situation. You talk of the glorious history of the Republican party! I talk of its glorious future. All that it has done is nothing as to its future possibilities. I believe in comparison with what it shall be, it is only a baby or a little bundle of political possibilities yet. Let us never cease to blow. Let us never haul down the American flag while there remains a political difficulty to be confronted or while there remains a political problem yet to be solved. The Democratic party in this city has made an effort indeed to put away Tammany. Cannot the Republican party improve herself? Cannot the party of Lincoln, and Garfield, and Blaine, and Grant, and Chase, and Sumner shake off the last remnant of bossism? (Applause.) We know that Adam started his administration well and Eve ran it out. Mr. President, would you have the forbearance, and you, gentlemen of the Republican Club, to only let me quote one line of the immortal Milton:

"The flowery Platt and the sweet rose of Eve."

We must advance, advance in a strength that is invincible and with a power that is literally without limit, advance to the consideration of currency, of financial questions, of questions of the laborer, of striking the exact balance between free trade and protection, an intensely difficult problem; and all the political and social woes of mankind on this hemisphere look to us for their renovation. The time has come for a great advancement.

If you are familiar with Walter Scott's novel of Ivanhoe, you will notice in the siege of the castle, you remember, just as Cedric was about to make his way into the opposing ranks there appeared before him a wretched old woman and said to him, "I am Saxon, do you know me?" "Know you?" said he, "you are Ulricka, the daughter of the Saxon lord of this castle, and, oh, you have lived as the concubine of Front de Boeuf, the Norman conqueror, and when your father and your brothers died defending their home and masses were said in every church in England, you were content to live in sin and in shame; contemptible hag, I wish I had my sword that I might kill you." But she replied, "However I have lived, I die well. When you see the red flag on the battlements, press the enemy's heart." On the next day the attacking party advanced under the leadership of the Black Knight, who was no other than Richard Coeur de Lion, and suddenly they saw the red flag on the battlements and descried a little blue smoke ascending from the castle roof—the hag had set the castle on fire, the storming party advanced, the awful blows of Richard Plantagenet were heard on the postern door, and in a short time the poor feudal baron was leveled to the ground. It is a time for present great advancement; I see the red flag, the signal for action. I see the blue smoke that indicates the combustion of our political companions curling up into the heavens. It is a time for the grand advance, and may the battle axe of Republicanism shiver in pieces all vestiges of party tyranny and lead us forward into the glorious, all-pervading freedom which under the leadership of that mighty party I believe we are permitted and decreed to attain. (Cheers and applause.)

"THE HOME OF LINCOLN."

Response by Dr. Emil G. Hirsch at a dinner of the Republican Club of New York, February 15, 1896.

Mr. President, the genius of the English language, said the Frenchman, was very peculiar, and I discovered that the Frenchman was right. I am to follow after one in whom Demosthenes and Cicero have found their resurrection (laughter), and another one whose wisdom and sound political philosophy justify his elevation to that highest chamber of American legislative bodies into which he will bring a little more than idle talk. I say I am to follow after. That makes me very uncomfortable, for to follow them I would have no hesitancy, their principles are mine, and whither they led I should go; but to follow after at a dinner like this makes me think of the old country parson who advertised as follows: "Wanted, a good stout horse to do a poor country minister's work." (Laughter.) I feel like advertising for a good, stout Republican horse, not another kind of donkey, to do my work here. If it were not for the fact that we Chicagoans are noted for our modesty (laughter), I should crawl into a hole. I may get there before I get through.

It is safe, Mr. President, to assert that to-day, four score years and seven after his advent, and more than three decades after his ascension to glory. Abraham Lincoln belongs to no one State. In the flesh the son of one nation, in the spirit he is proudly claimed and his memory is treasured as the priceless inspiration by all humanity. The whole earth is a willing pedestal to his fame, and the best and noblest of all nations asks for the privilege to garland afresh every year his memorial in their hearts. (Applause.)

In the alchemy of reverence for him the distinctions and differences of geographical longitudes or social hierarchy are dissolved. In royal palaces and baronial manors, museums, though oft they be of trophies won in days when America was still curtained from the ken of seafaring men, and monuments as they are of political systems antipodal to his, the name of the American railsplitter has become a household word, and by rulers is recognized as right to be one of their order, by a sanctification more solemn than heredity could ever confer (Bravo), and the common people untitled and unpurpled from pole to pole, and zone to zone, love and reverence the great American railsplitter. They know that he possessed the spirit of greatness, which comes to but the chosen few; they know that he loved the people and had faith in the national destiny of his own people, a faith that carried him through the fiery furnace of war and rebellion to his apotheosis, the last sacrifice on the altar of our reunited country. (Cheers and applause.) Still, though Lincoln to-day does no longer belong to one State or even to one nation, he has forever linked his name with the State and territory of Illinois. Every great man casts a lustre over the place where his cradle stood. His Mecca to-day is the magnet of all Islam. The patriarchs weave romance and reverence around the caves where their bones were laid to rest, and certainly there is one whose love was broad enough to encompass the whole world, who was so free from the limitations that are the heirlooms of all humanity in the flesh that he called himself the "Son of Man," even he, with a heart to which all humanity was pressed, has lent his name and glory to Bethlehem and to Galilee. (Applause.) And so the Bethlehem of Lincoln lies forever in history bathed in the flash of light of his own glory, and so does his Galilee forever find a place in the records of time. He was born in Kentucky. He came to our State at an early period of his life. It was there where he struggled with poverty, not material, but with poverty, spiritual and mental, and conquered the penury of his early days, and changed it by the power of his genius into a wealth unequalled by the learning of the most famous discoverers that search the stars or fathom the depths of the ocean. (Applause.) It was in Illinois that he first addressed his people from a stump and from the fence; it was in Illinois that he first practiced at the bar of an American Court of Justice; it was in Illinois that that tournament took place, the like of which no minstrel ever sung of, which awoke the Union to a realization of the danger that was approaching—the battle in which Douglass, a foe worthy of the steel of Abraham Lincoln, won the Senatorship, but from which Lincoln went forth to win the Presidency of the Nation at a time when the Nation needed that pilot sent to it by no lesser power than that which we call the power of God. (Tremendous cheering.) It was from Illinois that he set out for the capitol of the Republic, and to Illinois was brought back his mortality, there it sleeps under the very shadow of Illinois' own capitol. Illinois has been favored by the skies and the elements; her soil is rich; her rivers run swiftly; her industries, under Republican government, were active and thrifty; her chimneys many, smoking to heaven; the clanging of the hammer on the anvil is heard in many places; her hamlets are monuments to human ingenuity; her towns are bustling with energy, and her metropolis, ambitious to become the first city of the country, has acted as the representative of the Nation when the Nation invited all of her neighbors to come and witness the marvelous progress made since the days when Columbus discovered this continent, changing by her ambition a dismal swamp into a dream of beauty—the White City. Yes, Illinois, Chicago, has made glorious a bright page in the history of this Nation and of the world, and yet what is the coin that we find in the mines of Illinois? What are the wheat and the barley that grow there? What is the iron that is moulded and wrought there? What the planning, the plotting, the exchanges that are maneuvered in bustling Chicago? Yea, what is the new ambition of Chicago to make full of light the sooty atmosphere of her sky by kindling a new beacon of intelligence and education in her great university? What are all these possessions compared to the one priceless exceptional possession which it enjoys in the ownership of such names as Grant and Logan, as the Guard by the grave of Abraham Lincoln. (Great applause.) We in Illinois feel that such distinction entails new obligations, especially we of the Republican party of Illinois know that the Nation has the right to expect of us to be worthy of these hallowing memories. It is true that issues which convulsed the time and the age of Lincoln and Seward are decided forever, dead. The men that wore the blue and the men that wore the gray know but one flag, and with the Stars and Stripes waving over them they spring across the bloody chasm to grasp a brotherly hand and to register the vow to heaven that should ever that flag be assailed, either from within or without, the veterans from the blue field and the veterans from the gray belt will stand shoulder to shoulder, and conquer by their oft-proven heroism and valor the armies of the world for liberty and for freedom. (Applause.)

New duties await us, and new questions ask for solution. We Republicans of Illinois have no doubt that the Republican party with its glorious past has still a more glorious future before it. We know that patriotism, such patriotism as was Abraham Lincoln's, will be the solvent of all perplexities to-day. He was a politician. In these our days we associate with the word politician a sort of a by-meaning, and in consequence politics by the American people are regarded as something unworthy of the citizen of this land. In a Republic every citizen must be a politician as was Abe Lincoln. Private selfishness is sapping the very foundations of our political system. If it be, as Lincoln said, a government by the people, of the people and for the people, the people's will must be ascertained. No one has the right to disenfranchise himself. It is treason to the fundamental principles of our government to stay away from the ballot box and to take no interest in politics. (Great applause.) Of course, if politician is a synonym for coward, if politician means that by hook or crook the will of the people shall be defeated, then there is no word in the catalogue of any language so base as is the idea which is conveyed by that word, politician. But was this honest old politician of the old school a coward? He said in Illinois a country divided against itself cannot stand. A house divided against itself cannot stand. This country cannot be half slave and half free, and, thereby had the courage to endanger his chances for the Senatorial seat, but losing the toga of the Senator, he won the laurel wreath of glory and martyrdom in the chief magistrate's chair of the Nation. (Applause.) Our people want honest men. They want from the high place of authority to be instructed and to be guided, guided in the spirit of Abraham Lincoln. He was a patriot, patriot not of the jingo school, nor a patriot

of that school which is constantly looking about for a scapegoat. We have here in America a real scapegoat—the
foreigner. When we Americans commit any crime, the
foreigner stands ready to act as our shield, as the shield of
our sinless conscience.

I do not say aught against the stand taken by the orators who preceded me, that in Lincoln there asserted itself
the Puritan blood of his ancestral grandsire. To the Puritans this country owes a great deal. It is the Puritans
who have given to this country the backbone of its morality,
the unbending backbone sometimes, but if they had given
the backbone of our morality, still if this our country is too
large to be merely New England, it is the new world, and
all nations have contributed toward its wealth. In the Revolutionary days the Germans came to Germantown; the
Huguenots to the Carolinas; the Dutch to New Amsterdam.
All the nations of Europe contributed of their wealth to our
stores. And when old Abraham Lincoln called, in Illinois
more than five regiments marched to the song of "We are
Coming, Father Abraham," sung not in our English, but
in tones in the language of the Fatherland. When he called
they all rushed to the defense, and so to-day there is many
an American who does not know what that flag means, and
there are many who have not by their own choice, but by
accident, forfeited their hopes ever to act as Presidential
possibilities in the Republican party, who know, though
born across the briny deep, that among the symbols of the
world there are none so glorious as Old Glory, and who in
their household have no religious emblem to which they
ascribe such sacramental power as they do to the map of
the sky, the stars of the night, the bars of the light, and the
white of God's innocence. (Great applause.) To this
Americanism must be wedded the Republican party; the
Republican party must be wedded to principles that will
make our nation industrially independent, and every pledge
given by the Nation must be indeed redeemed honestly,

for no nation, and especially not a Republican nation, can afford to stand before the world a self-convicted, arrogant and impotent bankrupt. No. We must pay honestly all the pledges that we have ever entered into. (Applause.) To-day in America there is much talk about non-partisanship. An American must be a partisan. Abraham Lincoln was a partisan. Parties are necessary. Some parties seem to receive from God the providential mission to act as the constant No, the terrible negative, and there lies their province. As long as they confine themselves to that province they act for the good of the whole country, for they keep the positive party straight, for fear the old positive party, like old Israel, should wax fat and begin to kick, like so many instruments under God to make the Republican soreheads in exile come back purified and chastened (applause) to assume again the obligations of positive government. But a party that never knows what it is, and which only knows where it is at when offices are in sight, that party indeed can no longer be intrusted with the government of the Nation, longer than the rehabilitation morally of the Republican party requires. (Great applause.)

"THE REPUBLICAN PARTY."

Response by Hon. Joseph B. Foraker at a dinner of the Republican Club of New York, February 15, 1896.

Mr. Chairman, Ladies and Gentlemen:

I sincerely thank you for so kind, so cordial, and so complimentary a greeting. I wish I knew how, better than I do, to make fitting response to it. It seems to me all I can think of to say is simply, I thank you; and that I do with all my heart.

In undertaking to address you, I labor under at least two embarrassments. In the first place, I do not think I ever heard an abler, a more beautiful, a more appropriate speech than that to which we have just listened. (Great applause.) And it seems to me that the very best thing I could possibly do would be to move that we adjourn in order that the impressions made by that address might be left undisturbed upon our minds. Another embarrassment is that I recall, as I undertake to think of something to say in answer to this sentiment, that I once before addressed this same club upon this same subject, and told you then all I knew about it up to date; that cuts me off from the discussion, at least in large part, of the past of the Republican party. But perhaps that is as well as otherwise, for the past of the Republican party really needs that nothing should be said for it. It will take care of itself. It needs no eulogy. (Applause.) It is sufficient to say that it is replete with glorious achievements. The great days, and the great men of the Republican party of the past will forever challenge the admiration of the world. (Great applause.) And as the past is full of glory, so is the present resplendent with triumph. No political party ever before won such victories as we are now enjoying at the hands of those who defeated us, for, in the hour of their ascendancy, has come to us our most signal vindication. The Democratic party in power has been a sore trial for the country, but it has brought to all the rich blessings of experimental education. (Laughter and applause.) As a result, the people of this country know more than ever before of the relative work of Republicanism and Democracy. They know more about our principles and less about theirs. (Laughter.) It is no longer necessary, and there is a great saving in that when we come to the campaign oratory, to make an argument to demonstrate that if you manufacture a product abroad, you do not need to manufacture it here. (Laughter.) And even the most obtuse man can in the light of this experience comprehend that if other countries supply our wants the result is greater activity and prosperity for them, with corresponding idleness and distress for us. We have passed from the troubles of a surplus to the study of a deficit. (Laughter and applause.) We have seen our credit impaired, our currency deranged, and an endless chain of demands and evils, resulting in bond issues, bond syndicates, and bond scandals. (Laughter.)

Without an exception our home policy has brought only rack and ruin, while our foreign policy has been an uninterrupted chapter of disappointment and mortification. To make a long story short, three years of Democratic rule have demonstrated the heresy of Democratic principles, and established the wisdom and patriotism of ours. (Applause.)

They have done more. They have made it manifest that there is absolutely no harmony of opinion among Democrats as to what Democracy means. (Laughter.) You can scarcely find two of their leaders, who can be said to be in strict accord as to what constitutes the Simon pure article. (Laughter.)

They are hopelessly divided upon every great question. We have seen the House quarrel with the Senate; the Senate quarrel with the House; both Houses quarrel with the President, and the President refuse to agree with anybody. (Laughter.)

In the presence of the whole nation, and at a time of the most serious peril and grave responsibility, we have been treated to exhibitions of "party perfidy" and the "communism of pelf," while months passed with nothing done except to demonstrate incapacity to do anything at all, and now, finally, as a sort of grotesque climax to the whole miserable business, we have been called to witness the spectacular performance of the successor of John C. Calhoun, a Senator of the United States from the State of South Carolina, sah (laughter), standing up in his place in the most august place on earth, and in the name of statesmanship, to use his own language, "sticking a pitchfork into the big, fat ribs of a Democratic President." (Laughter and Applause.) Such experiences as these have made it painfully clear that great, rich, and powerful as our country is, there can be no prosperity unless wisdom, patriotism, and sound business sense are applied in the conduct of its affairs. (Applause.)

Everybody knows, and nobody better than the Democrats themselves, that the Democratic party lacks all these essential requisites of success. (Applause.) As a result, hundreds of thousands of them, preferring country to party, have bolted their organization, and cast in their lot with us. They voted with us last year, and they will vote with us this year. The elections of next November will triumphantly restore the Republican party to power, and the fourth of March, 1897, will mark the beginning of the second era of Republican rule. (Cheers.) One can speak with confidence of past events and of existing conditions. It is seldom that we can forecast without some misgiving the future, but it is safe to predict that certain things will come to pass when the Republican party regains control of the nation. It is safe, I take it, to assume that practically, without dissent or debate, there will be a revision of the tariff on protection lines (applause), to the end that our Government may have a sufficient revenue, and our industries and labor a sufficient protection. (Cries of "Good!") With equal unanimity, reciprocity will be restored and made a permanent feature of our commercial policy. With, perhaps, not so much unanimity, but with absolutely as much certainty, the high monetary standard Republicanism has ever represented will be upheld and the currency and banking systems well preserved and perfected. (Great applause.)

I pass all these matters by as undebatable, in order that I may have time left to speak a few words with respect to two or three other subjects, concerning which the Republican party will have a duty to discharge, about which there may not be so much unanimity, though I hope there may be. The first of these in both thought and importance is our merchant marine. (Applause.) This is a vast and a complicated subject, impossible to be elaborately discussed, or discussed at all, in any proper sense of the word, in an after-dinner speech. I do not refer to it, therefore, for the purpose of discussing it, but only that I may, if, happily, I may be able to do so, favorably attract attention to it. Speaking upon it in this way allow me to remind you that when our fathers had achieved our political independence, and had organized our government, they recognized that their work was not done. They at once undertook the work of securing our individual and commercial independence also. They succeeded. They accomplished their purpose by simply applying the principles of protection to both land and sea. We are all familiar with the wonders wrought in the development of our resources through the agency of protective duties on imports, but apparently only the limited few are aware that our achievements at home had their complete counterpart on the water. The basic proposition on which the fathers proceeded was that it should be made advantageous to carry goods in American-built ships. (Cries of "Good.") To that end they resorted to discriminating duties in tariff and tonnage. The result was a phenomenal development in ship-building and a marine that carried under the American flag at one time more than ninety per cent. of our imports and almost as large a percentage of our exports. But, as bad luck would have it, they had the theorist with them in that day as we have him with us in this, and then, as now, his favorite theme was free trade. He succeeded in persuading Congress to agree with him, and, as a result, by a series of enactments ending in 1828, the last vestige of protection for American shipping was removed.

The seductive phrase then employed was not "the markets of the world," or "tariff reform," but "reciprocal liberty of commerce." But it meant, as these modern phrases do, simply free trade—free trade on the ocean—and the application of the doctrine when made brought to American shipping the same blight that has ever attended the application of that doctrine in our experience. Decline at once set in, and thirty per cent. of our foreign carriage had been lost when the war came that swept away twenty-five per cent. more of it. The work of saving the Union and solving the great problems growing out of that struggle, the problems of emancipation, enfranchisement, reconstruction, and specie resumption, so pressed upon and occupied the Republican party that it had no opportunity to properly address itself to this subject until Mr. Cleveland's first administration was over.

Had President Harrison been re-elected, the probabilities are that something effective would have been done ere this; but he was not re-elected, and the tide had relentlessly run against us, until we now carry only twelve or thirteen per cent. of our foreign trade. It can scarcely be said that we have any longer an American marine. There are a number of views in which this is both discreditable and unfortunate. In the first place there is the patriotic view, the pride every American should feel in seeing his country's flag in all the waters of the world. And then there is the naval review, a nursery of seamen to man our battle ships in time of war; and then who can over-estimate the value of the employment it would afford to our people and our capital, or the indirect advantages that would result to us from the prestige it would give us in our trade relations.

But consider here for this evening only one feature of it, the direct indisputable financial results. Careful estimates show that we are paying annually more than one hundred and fifty millions of dollars in gold to foreign ships for the transportation of freight and passengers, every dollar of which should and would be paid to ourselves if our merchant marine was what it once was, or what, if we do our duty, it will be again. (Applause.)

It has been computed that within the last thirty years we have paid out in this way more than five times the amount of all the gold balances which we have been compelled to export. It has gone far enough. The time has come to change it. What is the remedy? A great many have been suggested, some good, some otherwise. I have no time here to enter upon the discussion of them, for the reasons I have already given you, and, therefore, I content myself with the simple declaration that the time has come for this great question to receive heroic treatment. Temporizing expedients will no longer answer.

The first starting point in the whole business is for us to plant ourselves upon the broad, underlying, patriotic proposition that we will not buy but build our ships. (Applause.)

The brand of America must be impressed upon every timber of every craft we sail (applause), and we must not relax our efforts until the United States flag again floats over ninety per cent. of our merchant marine. (Cries of "Bravo!") Some necessary bounties and subsidies and subventions are good enough in their way, but they are distasteful to the American people, and I have no faith in any policy that depends upon them. The practice of the founders of the Republic was wiser and better. Let us return to it. Let us profit by their wisdom and experience. Discrimination in tariff tonnage duties worked wonders once. It will do it again. Put bounties on American ships. Subject the free list of imports to the condition that they are brought into our harbors in American bottoms, under the American flag. (Applause.) Allow a rebate of ten per cent. on all dutiable goods of our own carriage. (Applause.) And when we come to a treaty of reciprocity, engraft upon it as one of its provisions that the goods mentioned in the treaty shall have the benefits of the treaty only on condition that they be carried in the ships of the reciprocating countries. (Applause.) Protect American marine insurance and American shipping from the tyranny, the oppression, the injustice that have been practiced by foreign marine insurance for the third of a century, and the work is done. (Applause.) But, says someone, there are treaty stipulations standing in the way of some of these suggestions. That is true as to some of them, but that only suggests the starting point in this patriotic work. We have experimented with this condition of things long enough. If there be anything standing in the way it must be modified or abrogated. That is our right; that is our privilege; that is our duty toward the American people. In short, it must be understood, and that is all I want to say about it, that America must be free to take, and hold, and enjoy her rightful place on the oceans that belong in common to all the nations of the world. (Great applause.)

And now, hand in hand with that, goes another duty, a duty that every patriotic heart should sanction, a duty that has been impressed upon us by recent events. We must not only recover our merchant marine, but we must have a navy able to protect it and to command respect for the flag wherever it is. (Great applause.)

And as a fit complement of an American marine and an American navy, we should at once build an American ship canal across Nicaragua. (Applause.) It is incomprehensible that the American people should have been content themselves until now, when sailing ships from the Atlantic to the Pacific coast to go ten thousand miles out of the way, around the Horn, through tempestuous seas, and inclement seasons. The commerce of the world demands the building of that canal, and if we do not build it somebody else will build it. Every suggestion of patriotism prompts and commends us to the work. (Applause.) We should not only build it, but control it. No one else should have any co-partnership in it with us. (Applause.) It should be open to the free use for all peaceful purposes of all other nations, subject to the condition that they pay such reasonable tolls as we may see fit to exact. (Applause.)

These, my Republican friends, not to detain you longer,

are three majestic works. They are worthy of the party that saved the Union and gave to immortality the great names of Lincoln and Grant. (Applause.) Their undertaking will be a fit crowning to the closing century, and their consummation will bring wealth, power, happiness, honor, glory, magnificence and grandeur to the American people, and so entrench the Republican party in the hearts of all this people that neither you nor I will live long enough to see another Democratic President. (Cries of "Good!" and applause, and "Three cheers for Foraker!")

"ABRAHAM LINCOLN."

Response by Chauncey M. Depew at a dinner by the Republican Club of New York, February 12, 1896.

Mr. President and Gentlemen:

Celebrations of the anniversaries of heroes and statesmen, of battlefields and significant events, have, as a rule, only an historical interest. They lack the freshness and passion of touch and attachment. It has always been the habit of peoples to deify their heroes. After a few generations they are stripped of every semblance to humanity. We can reach no plane where, after the lapse of 100 years, we can view George Washington as one of ourselves. He comes to us so perfect, full-rounded, and complete that he is devoid of the defects which make it possible for us to love greatness. The same is largely true of all the Revolutionary worthies, except that the Colonial Dames have raised— or lowered—Benjamin Franklin to the level of our vision by deciding that he was so human that his descendant in the fourth generation is unworthy of their membership. Thank Heaven, we can still count as one of ourselves, with his humor and his sadness, with his greatness and his everyday homeliness, with his wit and his logic, with his gentle chivalry that made him equal to the best-born knight, and his awkward and ungainly ways that made him one of the plain people, our martyred President, our leader of the people, Abraham Lincoln. (Applause.)

The Revolutionary War taught liberty from the top down; the Civil War taught liberty from the people up to the colleges and the pulpits. The Revolutionary struggle was the revolt of property against unjust taxation until it evoluted into independence. It was the protest of the leaders in commercial, industrial and agricultural pursuits against present and prospective burdens. Sublime as were its results, and beneficial as was the heritage which it left behind, there was a strong element of materialism in its genesis and motive. The Civil War threw to the winds every material consideration in the magnificent uprising of a great and prosperous people moved to make every sacrifice for patriotism, for country, and for the enfranchisement of the bondmen. The leaders of the Revolutionary struggle represented Colonial success. Washington was the richest man in the United States. Jefferson and Hamilton, Jay and the Adamses were the best products of the culture of American colleges and of opportunity. In the second period, when the contest was for the supremacy of the principle of the preservation of the Union against the destructive tendencies of State rights, Daniel Webster and Henry Clay represented the American farmers' sons, who had also received the benefits of liberal education. In the third period the protest against the extension of slavery—the war for the Union, with the contributions which came to our statesmanship from the newly settled territories, we had the heroes born in the log cabins. Their surroundings and deprivations were not those of poverty, but of struggle. The great leader was born in the log cabin. A little clearing in the wilds of Kentucky, a shiftless wandering to Indiana, and a repetition of the experience, another shiftless movement to Illinois, with no better results, a neighborhood of rough, ignorant, drinking and quarreling young men, and with no advantages of books, of household teachings, of church influences, of gentle companionship—these were the environments from which came, without stain, the purest character, the noblest, the most self-sacrificing and the loftiest statesman of our country or of any country. (Applause.)

The age of miracles has passed, and yet, unless he can be accounted for upon well-defined principles, Lincoln was a miracle. At twenty years of age, dressed in skins, never having known a civilized garment, he was the story-teller of the neighborhood, the good-natured giant who, against rough and cruel companions, used his great strength to defend the weak and protect the oppressed. He thirsted for knowledge, and yet was denied the opportunities for its acquisition, and he exhausted the libraries for miles around, whose resources were limited to five volumes, "Pilgrim's Progress," "Robinson Crusoe," "Weems' Washington," a short history of the United States, and the Bible. As a laborer upon the farm he was not a success, because he diverted his fellow-laborers from their work with his marvelous gift of anecdote and his habit of mounting a stump and eloquently discussing the questions of the day. As a flatboatman upon the Mississippi he was not a success, because, while he was among the class which delighted to call itself half-horse and half-alligator in the mad debauches on the route and in New Orleans, he was not of them. As the keeper of a country store he was not a success, because his generous nature could not refuse credit to the poor who could never pay. As a surveyor he was a failure, because his mind was upon other and larger questions than the running of a boundary line. As a lawyer he was successful only after many years of practice, because, unless he was enlisted for right and justice, he could not give to the case either his eloquence or his judgment. As a member of the Legislature of Illinois he made little mark, for the questions were not such as stirred his mighty nature. As a member of Congress he came to the front only once, and then on the unpopular side. The country was wild for war, or the acquisition of territory by conquest, and for an invasion of the neighboring Republic of Mexico. When to resist the madness of the hour meant the present, and perhaps permanent, annihilation of political prospects, among the few who dared to rise and protest against war, and especially an unjust one, was Abraham Lincoln.

The orators of all times have had previous orators for their models; but Lincoln formed his style by writing compositions with a piece of charcoal upon shingles or upon the smooth side of a wooden shovel, and copying them afterward upon paper. In this school, poverty of resources taught Lincoln condensation and clearness, and he learned the secret of success in appealing to the people—that is, directness and lucidity. Caesar had it when he cried: "Veni, vidi, vici!" Luther had it when he cried: "Here I stand; I can do no other; God help me. Amen." Cromwell had it when he cried to his soldiers: "Put your trust in God and keep your powder dry." Napoleon had it when, before the Battle of the Pyramids, he called upon his soldiers to remember that forty centuries looked down upon them. Patrick Henry had it when he uttered those few sentences which have been the inspiration of the school books since the Colonial days. Webster had it when he said, "Union and liberty, one and inseparable, now and forever." Grant had it when he said, "I will fight it out on this line if it takes all summer." And Lincoln had it when he drew to him his people and the men and women of his country by the tender pleadings of his first inaugural, by the pathetic, almost despairing, appeal of his second inaugural, and by that speech at Gettysburg which made every hero who had died a soldier again in the person of a new hero created to take his place by that marvelous invocation. He expressed in a single sentence the principle and the policy of the purchase of Louisiana, and the supremacy of the United States upon the North American

Continent when he said, "The Mississippi shall go unvexed
to the sea." He added to the list of his immortal utterances
which go down the ages to lead each new generation to
higher planes of duty and patriotism, "With malice toward
none; with charity for all."

The reception held by the President day by day was a
series of amusing or affecting scenes. He at once satisfied
and reconciled an importunate but life-long friend who
wanted a mission to a distant but unhealthy country by
saying, when all arguments failed, "Strangers die there
soon, and I have already given the position to a gentleman whom I can better spare than you." But when a little woman whose scant raiment and pinched features indicated the struggle of respectability with poverty, secured,
after days of effort, an entrance to his presence, he said:
"Well, my good woman, what can I do for you?" She
replied, "My son, my only child, is a soldier. His regiment was near enough our house for him to take a day
and run over and see his mother. He was arrested as a
deserter when he re-entered the lines and condemned to be
shot, and he is to be executed to-morrow." Hastily arising
from his chair, the President left behind Senators and
Congressmen and generals, and seizing this little woman
by the hand he dragged her on a run as with great strides
he marched with her to the office of the Secretary of War.
She could not tell where the regiment then was, or at
what place, or in what division the execution was to take
place, and, Stanton, who had become wearied with the
President's clemency, which, he said, destroyed discipline,
begged the President to drop the matter; but Mr. Lincoln,
rising, said with vehemence, "I will not be balked in this.
Send this message to every headquarters, every fort, and
every camp in the United States: 'Let no military execution take place until further orders from me. A. Lincoln.'"
(Applause.)

He called the Cabinet to meet, and as they entered

they found him reading Artemus Ward. He said: "Gentlemen, I have found here a most amusing and interesting book which has entertained and relieved me. Let me read from a new writer, Artemus Ward." Chase, who never understood him, in his impatient dignity, said: "Mr. President, we are here upon business." The President laid down the book, opened a drawer of his desk, took out a paper, and said, "Gentlemen, I wash to read you this paper, not to ask your opinion as to what I shall do, for I am determined to issue it, but to ask your criticism as to any change of form or phraseology," and the paper which he read was the immortal Proclamation of Emancipation which struck the shackles from the limbs of 4,000,000 of slaves. And when the Cabinet, oppressed and overwhelmed by the magnitude of this deed about to be done, went solemnly out of the room, as the last of them looked back he saw this strangest, saddest, wisest, most extraordinary of rulers again reading Artemus Ward.

To-day, for the first time since Lincoln's death, the twelfth of February is a legal holiday in our State of New York. And it is proper that the people should, without regard to their party affiliations, celebrate in a becoming manner the birth and the story and the achievements of this savior of the Republic. But it is equally meet and proper for us who are gathered here as Republicans to celebrate, also, the deeds and the achievements and the character of the greatest Republican who ever lived. This party to which we belong, this great organization of which we are proud, this mighty engine in the hands of Providence for the accomplishment of more for the land in which it has worked than any party in any representative government ever accomplished before, has its teachings and inspirations more largely from the statesmanship and utterances of Abraham Lincoln than from any other man. The first speech he ever made was a speech for that policy which was the first policy of George Washington, the first pol-

icy of the greatest creative brain of the Revolutionary period, Alexander Hamilton, the principle of the protection
of American industries. With that keen and intuitive grasp
of public necessity and of the future growth of the Republic, which has always characterized Lincoln, he saw in
early life that this country, under a proper system of protection, could become self-supporting; he saw that a land
of raw materials was necessarily a land of poverty, while a
land of diversified industries, each of them self-sustaining
and prosperous, was a land of colleges and schools, a land
of science and literature, a land of religion and law, a land
of prosperity, happiness, and peace. (Applause.)

Abraham Lincoln would draw the last dollar the country possessed and draft the last man capable of bearing
arms to save the Republic. He would use any currency by
which the army could be kept in the field and the navy
upon the seas. When the peril was so great that our
promise to pay only yielded thirty cents on the dollar, he
prevented the collapse of our credit and the ruin of our
cause by pledging the National faith to the payment of
our debts and the redemption of our notes and bills at par
in money recognized in the commerce of the world. The
Republican party stands for a policy which will furnish
abundant revenue for every requirement of the government,
and which will maintain the credit of the United States at
home and abroad up to the standard which is justified by
its unequalled wealth and power.

All hail the spirit, all hail the principles, all hail the
example, the inspiring example, of that man of the people,
that wisest of rulers, that most glorious of Republicans,
Abraham Lincoln! (Prolonged applause.)

"DINNERS."

Response by John B. Green, of New York, at a "stag" dinner of Commonwealth Council, R. A., at the Clarendon Hotel, Brooklyn, N. Y., in the winter of 1885-'86.

Mr. Chairman and Brethren:

If there is any subject upon which I have more qualifications to speak than another, it is dinners. My recollection runs not far enough into the past to say when my experience of dining began. I can only speak of Brooklyn for five years. Of government, my profession, and kindred topics, I have learned almost all that I know since my manhood began. I had to be taught to read before I knew anything of the "Press," and the "Army and Navy" were mere names to me, until one April morning nearly twenty-five years ago, my mother pinned a tri-colored rosette upon my jacket to show loyalty to the flag just fired upon by its own sons. Let me talk, then, of what I know best—eating was always natural to me. The only other subject of which I know anything like as much—"The Ladies"—is, fortunately for you and for me, committed to a wittier tongue.

It has been recorded that "the art of eating and drinking took its rise amid the mists of the remotest antiquity;" and that "its history is coeval with that of the race." There have been dinners that live in history: the banquet at which Cleopatra dissolved in wine a pearl worth a king's ransom, and the feasts of Lucullus will be remembered as long as Marathon and Waterloo—battles decisive of the fate of nations. Who does not recall mental pictures of the great baronial dining halls in the "stately homes of England," those schools of chivalric courtesy and gentle breeding? Many a deed the world has admired was inspired by the lessons learned there. There is the wounded knight borne back from the hot fight at Zutphen in that long struggle for civil and religious liberty in the Netherlands handing his water-flask, just lifted to quench his own raging thirst, to a dying soldier, with the remark, "Thy necessity is even greater than mine," and drinking his health afterwards. Yet Sir Philip Sidney learned this grace at the dinners in his father's hall. Poets have sung of dinners. A modern one takes his hero, summoned to go on with an old love before he is off with a new, over the blue Pyrenees, through some of the loveliest of national scenery, through a region rich with legends of the heroic age, and for the most part in company with a rival; to break forth at the end, not with love or jealousy; not of mountain peaks and sunny valleys; not of paladins and peers, the rent horn of Roland and his bursting nostrils, his sword cleaving the rock, but upon our theme:

> "O hour of all hours, the most bless'd upon earth,
> Blessed hour of our dinners!
>   The land of his birth;
> The face of his first love; the bills that he owes;
> The twaddle of friends and the venom of foes;
> The sermon he heard when to church he last
>   went;
> The money he borrow'd, the money he spent;—
> All these things a man, I believe, may forget,
> And not be the worse for forgetting; but yet
> Never, never, O never! Earth's luckiest sinner
> Hath unpunished forgotten the hour of his
>   dinner!
> Indigestion, that conscience of every bad stom-
>   ach,
> Shall relentlessly gnaw and pursue him with some
>   ache
> Or some pain; and trouble, remorseless, his best
>   ease,
> As the furies once troubled the sleep of Orestes."

When these lights have gone out and the melancholy gentlemen in dress suits, whose labors in serving us have compelled them to keep sober, regretfully agitate these soundless bottles and bottoms upward the glasses you have drained; when this joyous company, with clove-laden breaths, segregates in the cold grey morning, and its members seek repose, beside their indignant wives, may we be each ready to say, if asked, "Have you ever enjoyed a better dinner?" as was said, by a gentleman at an evening party, in reply to the exclamation of a bystander, "Well, did you ever see the like?" as a lady dressed in the lowest style swept by, "Never, that is, since I was weaned."

"THE LADIES."

Response by John B. Green of New York, at a banquet at Westfield, N. J., in celebration of her 100th birthday.

Some months ago, when the dinner committee notified the speakers of the toasts they were expected to respond to to-night, in common with the gentlemen who have already been heard, I began to write a speech that it might be ready for the dress rehearsal that was to have been had last Saturday night down at the North Avenue Hotel. I don't know why that rehearsal did not take place. I was unable myself to attend, in consequence of an important engagement with my nearest neighbor to organize in town a new club for the promotion of skill and recreation in the noble and scientific pastime of mumble-te-peg to fill a long-felt want in Westfield which existing associations are unwilling or lack the means to supply. I have understood, however, that Mr. Grogan objected upon the ground that he had to maintain a justly earned reputation for keeping a quiet, orderly place and could not afford to put it in jeopardy. He felt convinced that if as many people came together for any purpose in Westfield there was certain to be a row and he would not run any risk. So the project had to be abandoned, and you see the result in several of the speakers having taken double the time they should in delivering their addresses. The orators who did assemble on that occasion are said to have sadly made their way over to Mr. Shove's drug store, and with that recklessness of personal safety that characterized the urchin who was discovered one summer astride of a tombstone in a cemetery eating green apples and singing "Nearer My God to Thee," to have actually drank some of his soda water. I look upon that tale as apocryphal, as all of the chosen exhorters are here to-night apparently in perfect health.

With a flame-tipped pen that traced lines that burned holes in the paper as the blazing words sizzled from its nib, I set down my ideas in language that sparkled and coruscated iridescent with living color. I wrote about a yard and a half of speech filled with majestic thoughts that moved by stately marches, and in such brilliant array that the soaring eagle able to gaze unwinkingly at the noon-day sun could not look upon them without being dazzled.

Sad as it is to confess it, the truth must be told. I have parted with that speech. A listening world will hearken in vain for its dulcet tones. Its flute-like melodies are forever hushed. Tuned to lofty symphony its grand organ notes are silent for all time to come.

I was deaf to the claims of friendship when Geo. Peek solicited the MSS. to "paper the house" at his next club entertainment, because I knew that no matter how powerful the attraction he might offer now, after his outrageous assault on the etiolated morals of our sons and brothers, the indignant matrons and maids in town would not suffer their husbands and sweethearts to attend. And I sternly shut my ears to the pathetic pleadings of the editor-in-chief of the Standard who, in a voice trembling with emotion, begged me for the copy that his sanctum, now so cold and dreary under the depressing nightmare of Bill Peaseley's attempts at wit, might be lighted up with a cheerful glow; for I could remind your uncle Dudley that I had once in a moment of amiable weakness yielded to his request for copy, and he had no sooner got it in his office than it set fire to the place and destroyed the whole block. But there came an appeal that I could not resist. Mr. Sergeant wanted that

speech, and the king's request is a command, so with tears
in my eyes I surrendered. I sacrificed my only chance for
fame and your only hope of exhilaration at this feast of
reason without the flowing bowl. He wanted to blanket
through the winter a yard and a half of dog. Wrapped in
that rainbow hued mantle, that long stretch of blue Skye
perambulates the Boulevard nights, nobly supplementing
the deficiency of electric lights on that magnificent thor-
oughfare, until every Thomas and Maria in the neighborhood ceases courting and flees in terror from the unearthly
apparition; while the sober citizens of that side of the railroad track, who on rare occasions are kept out late by the
fascinations of fifteen-ball pool, as they wend their tortuous
way homeward, mistake the radiant vision for the aurora
borealis and wonder how those weird streams of rosy light
got so far south.

So I am here without a speech, and I hope you will
make in my behalf reasonable allowance for the marked
superiority of my fellow-speakers.

Fortunately, it is not customary on such occasions as
this to say anything about the sentiment that has been assigned one for a text. One is not expected to even allude
to his toast. You noticed that each of the speeches you
have just heard and enjoyed so much would have fitted as
well any other toast than the one it was hitched to. This is
not the fault of the speakers, because the men who write
the responses and supply them in New York at four dollars
a dozen seldom have a chance to see the toasts in advance
of delivering the ordered speeches. But apart from this,
postprandial speeches are all built on the model of Artemus
Ward's celebrated lecture on "The Babes in the Wood," in
which that renowned humorist made but one reference to
his subject, and that was when he closed an hour and a half
of talk on all sorts of topics by saying, "All this I might

have said had not the subject of my lecture been, "The Babes in the Wood."

Still I think I ought at least to say something upon the subject assigned me. I went a few days ago to the New York Bureau for supplying after dinner speeches in the Tribune building, and looked over the stock responses to the toast "Woman," but could not find anything that was not too distinctly Bacchanalian and Anacreontic to find favor here, and have despaired, knowing how uninspiring mineral water is. Yet I would not willingly subject myself to the crushing criticism of his opponent uttered by the God-like Daniel in the famous debate upon Foote's land resolution, when he said: "He has spoken of everything but the public lands; they have escaped his notice. To that subject in all his excursions he has not paid even the cold tribute of a passing glance."

It is more than two centuries and a half since Rare Ben Johnson put in the form you have it to-night the sentiment selected for me. It is twelve hundred years further back in time since Philostratus wrote: "Drink to me with your eyes alone. And, if you will, take the cup to your lips and fill it with kisses and give it so to me." But earlier than that the unrecorded sentiment had its birth, for the like thought must have thrilled the breast of Adam when for the first time in Eden, the eyes of the mother of our race looked in homage at her lord. And throughout the ages to come, so long as the sons of Adam woo the daughters of Eve, men will need no other stimulant to lofty purposes and noble deeds than that unspoken language of the eyes as soul greets soul when plighting their sacred troth. And we may believe, reverently, that if anything earthly is reserved in the life to come to minister to human happiness it will be those feelings which find expression as she drinks to him with her eyes and he pledges with his. I yield to none in admiration for this sentiment, but I must remind the dinner committee that the stimulant it refers to cannot be provided to order—cannot be bought with a price. It is a libation not poured out at every altar, it is a rare and precious draught whose price is above rubies. It is drunk but once in a lifetime and from a Holy Grail. And it is not in public that one lifts to his lips that golden chalice, but in the dearest spot on earth—home.

It is best typified by the romantic figure of She who has never unveiled her matchless beauty to any but the Kallicrates, for whose coming she waited in unchanging youth through two thousand years, hidden from the world in the seclusion of the caves of Kor.

And I think that the sweetest and most wonderful melody in the world is the tender song of the mother as she hushes her infant into slumber, but the music is caviare to the general. Most of us must be content with something lower, and to hear Patti at $5 a seat. But we will not fail to remember while we listen that the cantatrice of the concert hall is no more a satisfactory substitute for the diva than Apollinaris is for champagne. Pray pardon the comparison—I am treading on forbidden ground. I would not willingly offend you. My opinions as to what are the proper accompaniments of a public dinner are well known, and while I do not apologize for them, I assure you I am not a connoisseur of intoxicants. I am as ignorant of their baleful qualities as one of my reverend friends in town was a short time ago innocent of the mellow virtues of applejack.

As I dutifully went through the bill of fare, that we have all, I trust, much enjoyed, without having the opportunity of following St. Paul's advice to Timothy, I sympathized with a good bishop of my communion who had been entertained during one of his episcopal visits by a family of total abstainers, of whom he afterwards said that they gave him naught but water to drink as if he were a horse. But I noticed with pain and sadness that even in immaculate Westfield, the trail of the serpent is over it all. When Whittier wrote

> "So fallen! so lost! the light withdrawn
> Which once he wore!
> The glory of his gray hairs gone,
> Forevermore!"

he must have viewed with prophetic eyes this scene and thought of Westfield once proudly marching toward the chill heights of prohibition, now backsliding by a single weakness and heir to a lifelong remorse. Why! oh, why! was not that fatal sorbet left out of the menu? But for that one concession to civilization and cultivated taste none could have outstripped us in the race for cold-water honors where we were facile princeps. That sorbet was the golden apple dropped on purpose to stay Atalanta in her fleet progress toward the goal. Some other community more sternly virtuous will now take our stand upon a cairn of pure ice at the North Pole of total abstinence, and throughout the long polar night from her arctic eyrie alone survey the universe of stars.

"GEORGE WASHINGTON."

Response by John B. Green, Esq., of New York City, at a dinner in honor of Washington's birthday, at Westfield, N. J., February 22 1894.

We meet to commemorate the birth of him whose name is highest in the estimation of all Americans, and challenges the love and admiration of the rest of mankind, the general who commanded the soldiery of our people through the seven years of travail that ended when the greatest nation of the West was born—the statesman who guided that nation through its first years of its infant life—the patriot who then put aside all further civic honors, thereby furnishing a lasting example to his successors in power throughout remaining time—George Washington.

It has seemed to us especially fitting that this occasion

should be honored here and now; that the lesson of Washington's life should be more deeply graven upon our hearts. As there were kings before Agamemnon, so there have been heroes since Washington—Americans whose lives and achievements are justly held in honor in all our land, but the contemplation of the virtues of Washington and the recalling of the cause he served, are still profitable and in many communities necessary occupations.

We love and reverence Washington because he was the lapidary to whose labors we owe the brightiest jewels in modern civilized life—free thought, free speech, free men. Because he was the champion of the cause of the whole people, the liberty of the individual.

The world loves a good soldier and admires a brave man, but it will cherish the name of Washington long after it has forgotten those of Alexander, Farnese, John Churchill and Richard Neville. The Prince of Parma was a more accomplished soldier, yet his military talents were enlisted in behalf of the most intolerant bigot that ever from a throne made war upon his subjects. The Duke of Marlborough, who never fought a battle that he did not win, nor beleaguered a town that he did not take, was a more successful general, but his victories were won only that the balance of power in Europe might be maintained, an idea of importance to none but monarchs. And Warwick, the king-maker, was surely not less courageous, when last of the barons, knowing the battle was on to the death, his sword drank the life-blood of his war horse, as he flung away his scabbard, on that beautiful Easter day in 1471, when feudalism made its final stand on the fatal field of Barnet.

So long as human nature is what it is, we will need the inspiration of Washington. There were many men who gave their lives and fortunes for civil and religious liberty in the Netherlands, but of only one, William the Silent, has history written that he "labored to produce mutual respect among conflicting opinions when many dissenters were as bigoted as the orthodox and when most Reformers fiercely proclaimed not liberty for every Christian doctrine, but only a new creed in place of 'all the rest.'" The people of England who suffered for conscience sake the fires of Smithfield were not thereby made more humane toward the Puritans, and almost the first public act of the Pilgrim Fathers, whom we laud so highly, after seeking in bleak New England freedom to worship God in their own way, was to drive Roger Williams forth into the wilderness for desiring the same liberty for himself.

We cherish the hope that the times have made persecution for opinion's sake obsolete, and your presence here, with your varied views of life and duty and mutual respect for your differences, prove the hope is not vain.

Remember how much we owe to Washington for this happy state of affairs. It is a long time from Galileo to Tennyson, but the distance that measures the course of freedom through the years that have flowed between them is greater still. Where the older poet of science timidly ventured to say that the world moves the later minstrel sings, "Let the great world spin forever down the ringing grooves of change." Go with the planet as it swings its airy course, lighted by the sun of progress, or be crushed beneath its mighty mass as it rolls irresistibly forward.

"DANGER AHEAD!"

Response by Henry Wollman, of Kansas City, Mo., at the second annual banquet of the Commercial Law League of America, at Omaha, Neb., August 18, 1896.

Mr. Toastmaster: Politeness and vanity prevent me denying your statement that I am a great after-dinner speaker, but candor compels me to admit that I am neither an agreeable nor cheerful "before-breakfast talker." The clock shows that the breakfast hour is nearly here. I must confess that I am usually very cross and surly before breakfast, so you must prepare to suffer.

I feel grateful to you for the very prominent position you have given me upon this programme. I have been taught that the two most important places upon a banquet programme are the opening and the closing speeches, and consequently I feel highly flattered that you have asked me to respond to the closing toast. I beg you, Mr. Toastmaster, not to shatter my conceit by telling me that it was not done by design, but that in the "shake-up" it just happened to come that way. Let me return to Kansas City believing it was an honor accorded to me as a tribute to merit. I desire to tell my friends at home in the strictest confidence, that where I was the least known I was the most appreciated, as we are told was the case with prophets in the time of the Bible.

I regard this as one of the greatest opportunities of my life. It certainly is a rare occasion where a man can talk to the gentle sex and have them situated so they can't talk back. Remembering that I am still a bachelor, you can readily understand how thankful I am for an opportunity to address an audience, among whom are such lovely young women as I see before me. Recently I delivered an address to three hundred unmarried school teachers, young and old, but for some unexplained reason I have since found to my sorrow that I sowed my seed on fallow soil, and that I would have to try farther from home, so following out the old lesson that is always read to bachelors about a "faint heart and a fair lady"—I am here. I feel that tonight, with so many generous and charitable young women in my audience, I certainly must succeed, for should I make a good speech, some girl, braver than the rest, will certainly accept me out of a spirit of admiration. Should I fail, I know that in the kindness and the loving sympathy of

the sex, she will take me, because she pities me. So
whether I fail or succeed at speech-making, I shall have advanced my matrimonial prospects.

I was told by a friend to-day that the reason I was put
upon this programme, was because I was said to be such
a witty man. After I entered this magnificent banquet hall
and read the sentiment affixed to the subject assigned to
me, I felt certain that that must have been the reason. I
am confident, that sentiment could never have been given
to any but a witty man. Think of a real wit talking in
anything but a bright and happy vein on that exceedingly
cheerful subject, "Danger Ahead."

If you don't think that it is very funny, Mr. Toastmaster, when you return to your hotel, arouse your little boy
from his peaceful slumbers and say, "Charlie, wake up,
there's danger ahead!" and see how he will brighten up,
and how long he will laugh. To-morrow, as you pass down
the street, walk up to three or four men and say to them,
"Stop! there's danger ahead," and see how gleefully they
will smile and how much of a joke they will think there is
in the announcement.

Mr. Toastmaster, you treated the others better than you
did me. As I look at the programme, I find that nearly all
the other subjects call for happy and witty responses, but
mine, "Danger Ahead"—not in a thousand years.

There's "The Uncertainty of the Law"—it pours joy
and happiness and brings smiles and laughter eternal into
the household of every lawyer. It gives us our bread, our
meat and drink. Through it we convert the darkness of
other people's despair into the sunshine of our own lives.

"The Making of the Law." That is one of the funniest
subjects ever given to anybody in seriousness. Every man
who goes to the Legislature regards it as a jolly vacation in
a sunny clime. We, who are called upon to construe the
laws, know that most of them must have been conceived in

a spirit of playful humor. It has often been said, too, that gladdening things have touched the palms of legislators. For my part, I can't believe it; and yet I must admit that I never saw a sad or sorrowful face in a legislative chamber.

"Lawyer and Client." A lawsuit is a circus, the judge is the ringmaster, some of the lawyers are the bareback riders doing the daring feats that attract the crowd, while others of the lawyers take in the cash at the box office—the litigants are said to be the clowns, at whom the concourse laughs—and there's the humor of it.

"Law and Justice." Now, isn't that a joke? It may not strike you that way at first, but think of it—law and justice, side by side. When the toastmaster locked law and justice in the same room, he did it to be funny. He saw there must be a bloody fight, and he enjoys the sight of blood.

"Law, a Progressive Profession." I have heard of progressive consumption, and I have always been told that a man who has a first-class lawsuit had a case of progressive consumption. I can't imagine what that subject means, unless it is, that it is a misprint on the programme, and should have read, "Law, a Progressive Consumption."

"The Commerce of the Seas." That refers to the business of issuing attachments and replevins and other dreadful writs, under which commercial lawyers "seize." There is no humor in that subject—for the defendant; it is always tragic for him, unless he knows you are coming, and then you know the rest. But even then it is still tragedy—only there is a change of tragedians.

"The Conservatism of the Bar." Every lawyer's life training makes him conservative, and from the awful examples that he constantly sees of the direful failures of those who are not conservative at the bar, he concludes that while liquor and champagne brighten, exhilarate and set us aglow, continuous happiness is brought about by very moderate drinking, or what you, in polite language, would call conservatism of, or at, the bar.

"The Ladies." At a lawyers' banquet that always refers to mothers-in-law. The mother-in-law has been the cause of many a lawsuit. No lawyer could afford to pass through life without expressing his intense gratitude to the mother-in-law, for she has furnished our profession, directly and indirectly, so much profitable and high-class business.

"The Press." Aye, there's the rub! Whether the press produces gladness and joy, depends a good deal on the object of the press. If she be kind and loving and manifests her belief in reciprocity, then the "press," I am told, is delightful. But if, perchance, she should resent the "press"— oh! then the result would be awful to contemplate. Your refuge then would either be a lawyer to keep you from a dungeon vile, or to a doctor to restore your Apollo-like face to its accustomed beauty—as near as may be. The press is not altogether a witty and humorous subject. Whether it is or not, I would say, depends entirely upon the "pressee."

And now, Mr. Toastmaster, you can see how unfairly you have treated me by giving everyone else a subject out of which there may be extracted some humor, pleasure or profit, while you have given me a heavy tragedy subject, out of which to extract some wit.

(Mr. Wollman concluded with a dissertation, in a more serious vein, on the subject and danger of judges accepting passes or other favors from corporations, or in any way allowing themselves to get under obligation to influences that would give the public the slightest excuse for believing that they were prejudiced in their decisions, and urging that they should keep themselves, like Cæsar's wife, "above suspicion."—Ed.)

SPEECH OF JOHN B. GREEN,

President of the Brooklyn Republican League, at the dinner in honor of the birthday of Abraham Lincoln, at Remsen Hall, Brooklyn, N. Y., February 13, 1888.

Gentlemen: We meet as partisans, frankly avowing our allegiance to the Republican party, our abiding faith in its purposes, our conviction that it is the best existing instrumentality for securing to the American people the blessing of good government. We meet to commemorate the birth of the greatest of our fellow-partisans—the Liberator and the Martyr. Of him who was at once the foremost Republican and the first patriot of his time—Abraham Lincoln. His fame is a national possession, but in a special sense ours. Time has not made Thomas Jefferson the less a Democrat, nor his great rival, Alexander Hamilton, other than a Federalist. And as the ages flow onward it will be as impossible to transform Abraham Lincoln into anything but a Republican as it will to change Samuel J. Tilden into an Abolitionist.

Inspiring as the theme is, it is not mine to linger upon. To lips more eloquent and minds attuned to grander harmonies be left his eulogy, mine the lighter duty to bid you cordial welcome here and to extend the League's hospitality to her distinguished guests.

The Brooklyn Republican League is the handmaid of the Republican party. She believes that the aggregate of the members of that party is wiser than any member of them. She nominates no candidates, but when they are nominated she makes their cause her own. She says to the great organization whose daughter she is, as Ruth did to Naomi, "Whither thou goest, I will go; where thou lodgest, I will lodge; and thy people shall be my people."

We are entering upon the quadrennial contest for the greatest political prize on earth. Let us indulge the hope that it will be waged upon principles rather than about personalities. That whosoever either party selects will be tried by the record, aims and policy of his party; that the nominee of our opponents will not claim the suffrages of his fellow-citizens because of his superiority to his associates or the enemies he has among them. Are the tendencies and professed principles of Democracy indefensible that its apologists claim consideration for its candidates on the score of personal merit? The plan of every recent Democratic campaign—lesser as well as greater—has been predicated by an affirmative answer to this question. The local Democracy entered the lists last fall with a champion clad in the shining armor and flying the blue pennant of reform. His heralds loudly trumpeted his resisting power to the sinister influence which entered him. Beside him, hooded falcon at the tourney, perched the "Eagle," its bandage only loosed for it to peck at the adversary. The tilt was won and the knight received his guerdon and the royal command: "The tax collector must go; the fire commissioner must stay." Submission must not only be unconditional but conspicuous. In the first month the white flag of surrender floated over the municipal citadel and the McLaughlin arms were replaced over the portals of the City Hall. If in the ensuing two years legitimate enterprise would enter Brooklyn, let it lay its tribute of blackmail at the feet of the freebooters who hold the fortress or remain without the walls. Shall the surplice and cassock obscure the electric light? Is character, abilities, and exalted social position in a civil service commission, when the civil service has for two years been "pressed down, shaken together and running over" with political vassals, a compensation for the alliance that has given a renewed term to the Board of Excise? Does a polished address and professional learning only fit a corporation counsel for a secret envoy extraordinary to the court of Gambrinus?

But there are reforms that we are to have. There are more voters than ever in Brooklyn, therefore they should have another day to register in. Then, tell me, gentlemen, the reason for putting the extra day nearer election when the time now intervening is scant for the publication and scrutiny of the lists. The preservation of the ballots is a constant temptation to dispute a count which should be indisputable. Then make the count indisputable. It ought not to be possible for any quartette of scoundrels to nullify the will of the people and destroy the evidence of their guilt. When venal, ignorant or drunken canvassers in the slums can wait for orders, delay returns until directed what to make them, there should be at hand the means of proving and correcting their crimes or mistakes. Seal the boxes the moment the polls close, send them at once, with the poll-lists, under guard, to a central station; open none until all arrive; count all at once; make public proclamation and certificate of the result, and then burn the ballots.

The Democratic party sometimes boasts that it has long maintained its Protean character under the same masque, while it reproaches its rival with being the young offspring of a dire necessity, the conception of a great cause, even now overtaken by a senile decrepitude. But Truth is everlasting, a principle is eternal; only the methods of search for the one and the application of the other change. The independence of communities and national unity were as much involved when Arminius met and overthrew the hitherto unconquered Roman legions under Varus near the head waters of the Ems, as the former was when Brooklyn claimed a home-rule charter, and the latter was when General Sherman marched to the sea. And when the English barons with Stephen Langton at Runnymede wrested from King John the great charter, the monarch's signet was the archetype of the signatures to our own declaration of independence, and in it was the potentiality of that signature in our own time that emancipated four millions of bondmen.

If the Republican party, my brothers, proud of and cherishing the heritage of an illustrious past, but holding fast to sound principles and facing forward, under standard-bearers from its best blood, brain and character, shall contest the vital issues of the present, its past defeats, as the touch of the earth to Antaeus, will infuse new strength in its sinews, and out of the next conflict it will come to find the Democracy, like Attila after Chalons, upon its heap of Confederate saddles and surrounded by its own spoils ready to light its own funeral pyre.

"OUR COUNTRY."

Response by Frank T. Lodge, of Detroit, Mich., at Decoration Day banquet, held at Detroit, Mich., May 30, 1893.

Mr. Toastmaster, Ladies and Gentlemen:

I am greatly embarrassed at rising to respond to this sentiment, not from a lack of appreciation of the length, and breadth, and depth of the subject, nor for a lack of love of the thing for which it stands, but on account of my inability to properly sound for you the swelling chords of music, of sentiment, and of eloquence which could be struck out of such a subject as this by one older and more eloquent than I. To-day, all over this broad land, all over the sturdy North, and, I am glad to say, in many places in the redeemed South, loving hands have strewed flowers over the graves, eloquent tongues have spoken in praise, and musical voices have sung paeans in memorial laudation of the fallen heroes, to whom the sentiment, "Our Country," meant a loyal love that shot and shell and blood and pain could not quench. And there are in this audience men who, from the deep stores of that five years' terrible experience, could tell you, in words far more graphic than mine, that to them, at least, the sentiment, "Our Country," means something that called for the surrender of all the ties of family, of home, of fortune and of fame; and still it was a sacrifice that was gladly made.

And yet, my friends, I feel that to no one more than to the young men and women of to-day should this sentiment, "Our Country," mean more. There was a time when life in this country meant privation and toil. It meant stern, hand to hand struggles with the unsubdued wilderness. It meant hardship and sacrifice. It meant Indian midnight massacres. It meant desolated hearthstones. It meant none of the comforts and luxuries which we have here to-day. Yet, prompted, as it was, by a love of freedom, full of toil and terror as it was, our forefathers were content to suffer, and Washington and his soldiers at Valley Forge were the most eloquent response and the highest expression of loyalty which that mystic sentiment, "Our Country," will ever produce.

Later on, when our country was in the wrong, when she engaged in a war of conquest, and wrested from a weaker government thousands of her broad acres, the sentiment, "Our Country, right or wrong," prompted many to rush into danger and face death and wounds that our country's flag should not come down in defeat.

But the culmination of loyalty, the grandest sacrifice that any country ever made, was when the liberty lovers and patriots of our land rose up with unselfish devotion to purge our country of the plague of slavery.

A large portion of this audience were babes in arms, and many of us were born long after the storm of civil war swept over this land.

To us the war is not even a memory. But, through the enlightening influence of the public schools, through the blessings of an education that is widespread and almost universal, I believe that love of country and loyal patriotism is as strong to-day as it was on the day when the first gun fired on Sumter raised a storm of cleansing that shook our nation to its very foundations.

For this I thank the public schools; and, to-night, if you ask me what is the cornerstone of our country's welfare at the present time, and for all time to come, I shall say it is our public schools. To me the first thought, therefore, that is evoked by this sentiment is that we firmly establish a carefully nourished and protected system of public schools to which every child in our broad land must be sent.

Napoleon said that the future of France rested in her mothers; that the hand that rocked the cradle ruled the world. True it is, that the hand that controls, and the brain that directs, the education of our children marks out the lines upon which the future of our country must be reared. If our public schools are broad and liberal, unbiased and impartial, seeking only to bring our children face to face with the great truths in nature, history and literature, they will graduate from their halls to become the citizens of to-morrow, broad-minded, liberty-loving and patriotic men and women. If our educators are illiberal and prejudiced, or feeble and weak; if our education is restricted to the few, and the children of the many grow up in ignorance, our jails and almshouses will be full, and the high places of our nation's patriotism will be empty indeed.

The second thought which my sentiment strikes out for me is that our country must be free from class distinctions: it must be the home, not of Germans, nor of Irish, nor of Italians, nor of Poles, but of American citizens, men who were born and nurtured here, and who have drawn in the air of liberty with their vital breath, together with men who have renounced allegiance to any and to every potentate, and who find in the Stars and Stripes their only allegiance and their only shield.

To-day, my friends, this country has no gloomier menace than the unrestricted hordes of ignorant, poverty-stricken and criminal classes who are daily pouring across our borders; and it will require strong brains and steady hands to guide our ship of state through the storm that is already lowering upon us. Our first attempt at restricted immigration was a dismal failure, and should bring the blush of shame to the cheek of every patriot. Weak-kneed politicians have basely truckled to the clamorous shout of Kearneyites and sand-lot agitators, themselves foreigners, and have disregarded treaties and broken contracts, which, were they made with stronger nations, would, long ere this, have called fleets of war to prey upon our coasts and make us respect our solemn contract obligations.

What we want is honest restriction; what we want is patriotic, careful consideration of such subjects. We ought to make admission to citizenship in the United States a badge of honor, and not merely a token that another voter has been added to the ranks of the great unwashed.

Last year, in Westminster Hall, in London, a fog so thick as almost to obscure all objects descended upon the city and filled the halls of Parliament, so as to make it difficult to transact business there. A committee of sanitary engineers were appointed to see if they could remedy the difficulty, and very soon the members noticed that inside the Parliament chambers the atmosphere was as clear as that of the open country, while outside it was as murky as before. Struck with the change, some of them investigated the methods by which it had been effected. Descending to the basement, they saw, stretched across the opened windows, sheets of cotton covered with filth, slime and mud. Through these sheets, which had been previously wet, the air was forced into the Parliament building. The air was purified, but the cotton, which had previously been as white as snow, was covered with the filth; and, upon analysis, many of the most deadly microbes and bacteria were discovered to have been imprisoned in it.

We have welcomed to our shores the oppressed of every clime, because, with our Christian institutions, our churches and libraries and public schools, we have thought that we could christianize and elevate these abandoned hordes and make of them good citizens. We may succeed, my friends, in ameliorating their condition, but the filth that is being precipitated upon us must be deposited somewhere. The body of our citizens who were here are like the snow-white cotton; while they purify what has passed through them, they themselves retain the germs and filth which are left behind. To-day, the problem of immigration confronts us with sterner menace than ever before. It is being thundered at us from the platform. It is being preached at us from the pulpits. It fills the columns of our public press; but we still slumber on in fancied security, trusting —as most Americans do—to luck, while we continue to send foreign saloon-keepers and pothouse boodle politicians to make laws which enlarge the privilege of this very class, and it is only through such organizations as this, of patriotic, intelligent, public-spirited citizens, that the evil can ever be remedied. God bless their work and speed their efforts!

You all know the story of the soldier of the empire, into whose body the surgeon in the hospital was probing for the bullet which had penetrated very near his heart. Those were the days before they had chloroform and other anæsthetics to deaden the pain of surgical operations. Writhing in pain as he was, as the surgeon's knife cut deeper and deeper, he looked up into his face and smiling said, "Just a quarter of an inch more, doctor, and you will touch the emperor." I long for the time when we can, with equal truth, say to him who comes near our hearts, "Just a quarter of an inch more and you will touch our country." If we cannot truthfully say it now, we can be educated to it. God bless our public schools! The flag that floats over every one of them in this broad land teaches our youth to reverence the banner of our country, and should a crisis ever come which requires a solid phalanx to rally for its defense against any foe, their myriad hosts will consist almost entirely of the graduates of our public schools, who have every day seen floating over them the flag of the free, and upon whose hearts has been emblazoned in characters of living light the broadening, the elevating sentiment, "Our Country."

"PRESIDENT GRANT AND SAN DOMINGO."

Response by Congressman William Alden Smith of Michigan, at the annual banquet of the Middlesex Club of Boston, Mass., in honor of the birthday of Ulysses S. Grant, Saturday evening, April 27, 1895.

Mr. President:

Permit me to thank you for the kind invitation so generously extended by the committee of arrangements to meet with you upon the anniversary of the birth of one of America's most distinguished sons, and one of the world's greatest men. We have met for the purpose of honoring the memory of Ulysses S. Grant, the luster of whose life lights up the entire field of human action with a glow and fire of perpetual glory, unclouded by time and undimmed by circumstance. To single out of his inspiring life its greatest achievement, is a task I have not undertaken. His early struggles are an inspiration; and his maturer life, with its responsibilities and severe trials, a benediction. Modest, genuine, frank and tender; firm, heroic, thoughtful and wise, possessing that charm so rare in the public man of to-day, golden silence—he could nevertheless break it with such intelligent speech as would command the respectful attention of the people of any land.

The artists of France were astonished a short time ago when the spirit of Raphael, Angelo and Titian re-asserted itself in the genius of Fritel, whose brush strikingly portrayed the rulers of the past. He burst the boundaries of his profession and entranced the eye of the critic with a master painting, illustrating the march of empires and the leaders of men. First, Julius Cæsar, haughty, proud, imperious, his face radiant with the superb victory of Pharsalia, where his imperial eagles found new standards; then Rameses II; next Hannibal the Carthagenian—Tamarlane the Tartar. At the left of Cæsar, Napoleon rode, flushed with the victories of his Italian campaigns; dauntless as at Austerlitz, Marengo or the Alps—then Alexander the Great, and next rides Charlemagne, as proudly as when "in the ancient metropolis of the world and in the fullness of his fame Pope Leo III. placed the crown of Augustus upon his brow and gave him, amid the festivities of Christmas, his apostolic benediction." Onward they ride, at the head of the armies, testing the perspective of the picture. The old world marveled at the daring intrepidity and skill of these great leaders of civilization's advancing march. Yet many of them ruled but to ruin. Not one of them left that fragrant memory characteristic of those who participated in the nobler drama of American liberty and enfranchisement.

Washington and his contemporaries fretted under the galling yoke of English oppression, and the revolution expressed and emphasized the higher aim and purpose of mankind.

Lincoln's simplicity and naturalness, coupled with his uncompromising love of humanity, prompted the second scene in the great drama of the new world.

Grant's unequaled valor, determination and strategy brought to a final and everlasting conclusion a civil strife which was destined to cement in one bond of fraternal union this vast empire.

Oh, artist of the future! Group these three tender memories, kindle the fire of human liberty, and enlighten future ages with this latest and grandest ideality!

Our national military school taught Grant the value of strategic points of defense and attack. His campaigns were marvels of exactness and keen perception, executed with prowess and true military genius.

It is not my purpose to traverse these scenes, but to take up another phase of his public career, of which the younger generation knows so little. Shortly after his election as chief executive, President Grant concluded the negotiation with the Dominican Republic, begun by Secretary Seward. His keen appreciation of the advantage of American ownership and control of the island of San Domingo was in line with his record so amply demonstrated in the field of military triumph. He promptly decided that it was wise for the American nation to accept this island, which was offered freely by its inhabitants, and submitted a treaty of annexation, which, however, failed of ratification by a tie vote in the Senate.

The acquisition of San Domingo he believed to be a strict adherence to the Monroe doctrine—a measure of national protection. It had been important from the formation of our government that the American nation control, as far as possible, the West Indies. Our Presidents have expressed an almost universal desire of the people for an advanced naval outpost between the Atlantic coast and Europe. Nearly all of the early statesmen have agreed that the West Indies naturally form a part of the North American territory, and should be absorbed ultimately by the continental states.

President Grant set his heart on the annexation of San Domingo, because of its value to our country, and its prominence among the West Indies. The overtures for annexation came voluntarily from the people of that blood-drenched island, who sought political affiliation with us because they believed it would save them from the daily and hourly conflict with the Haytian people. They realized that they were but the toys of ambitious chieftains who obtained and maintained their power in the island through strife. They turned to the United States, believing that our government could extinguish lawlessness by firm and judicious measures of administration. The question of accepting this free gift, which any government of Europe would have seized eagerly, was a patriotic privilege of which President Grant knew the value.

The world could have said that if the Haytian spirit of lawlessness was to dominate the island, its effects upon the Antilles would be demoralizing, while prosperity and good government in San Domingo would have its effect in subduing civil strife. The Dominican people longed for a higher and better citizenship. They had fought for and established their government against oppression and conquest. That fact should have attracted the favorable commendation of the people of our country. Their government was constitutional, presided over by a patriotic president, three times regularly chosen for his personal qualifications of intelligence and patriotism. After thus serving the people, when insurrection was incited again, they urged President Baez to accept an absolute dictatorship over the island. This he refused in so patriotic and inspired an utterance as deserves a place among the literary classics. These petty and aggravating insurrections along the Haytian border led thoughtful men in the island to look abroad for relief. People of all classes asked that the strong arm of this nation be thrown around them, putting an end to the efforts and hopes of seditious revolutionists. They knew of the sacrifices made in the civil war to unfetter the slave, and turned to us as a Mussulman turns toward Mecca.

Why did we not accept this gift?

Was not the island advantageously located?

Was it not inhabited by patriotic people?

Was it not rich in natural resources?

Our commission of inquiry said that the condition of

the Dominican was far better than could have been anticipated, that high crimes were comparatively unknown, that
no pauper class existed, that intemperance and beggary
were more common among the enlightened nations of the
world. The people were described as courteous, respectful
and polite, kind and hospitable; desirous of educational
advantages, and a higher citizenship. The resources of
their country were vast and various, and, in the opinion of
the commission, San Domingo is one of the most fertile
regions on the face of the earth. Fanned by trade winds,
they were more fortunate than the islands further within
the Gulf, constantly supplied with pure air from the sea.
The Bay of Samana was the most important in the West
Indies. It is thirty miles long and ten miles broad, com-
modious enough to accommodate the largest fleets.

Why do we need this island? For this good and sufficient reason: It sits like a sentinel in the Caribbean Sea,
guarding the Mona Passage, destined to be the Eastern
avenue of communication between the two great oceans
when the Nicaragua Canal shall be an accomplished fact.

Our relations with the West Indies, Central and South
America are growing closer and more important every year.
Should we not have an intermediate point from which the
United States could reach their objects of trade and enterprise? Such a point is this island, containing 22,212 square
miles—larger than Massachusetts, Vermont, Rhode Island
and Connecticut. A trained military eye could appreciate
the importance of this outpost, and President Grant would
have made it a part of the American Union. How clearly
he saw, how courageously he acted, and with what patriotism was he inspired. This is the age of trade conquests
the world over. The countries of the Western Hemisphere
stand face to face with the necessity of dealing with one
another as Americans. This entire group of magnificent
islands is naturally a part of the American territory. "The
West India Sea corresponds to that of the Mediterranean

from Syria to the pillars of Hercules. The Mediterranean is divided into an eastern and western basin, and as Italy, Sardinia and Tunis divide the basin there, so Cuba, Jamaica, San Domingo and Yucatan divide the Gulf and the Carribean Sea. As the former is fed by the venerable ancient Nile, so ours is augmented by the pulsating artery of the Mississippi. The Mediterranean is a world sea, lying in the temperate zone, amid an ancient civilization, and our southern basin is destined to be a world sea when an international waterway shall pierce the isthmus connecting the Eastern and Western Hemispheres by direct and rapid communication."

This has been the dream of trans-Atlantic thinkers for two hundred and fifty years. Indeed, its importance was suggested by Charlese V., after the discovery of America by Columbus, and later by Philip II., to whom Cortez reported that the greatest service he could render to the king was to find an opening through the isthmus to the Pacific. Lack of funds and an ignorant superstition caused this work to be abandoned because, as was said: "God had advisedly separated the two oceans by land in order to curb the fury of the waves." The idea of constructing a canal through Lake Nicaragua was first suggested in 1665. Thus we see why England always has been alive to the importance of island ownership and territorial acquisition in the vicinity of the isthmus. Its construction will raise the islands to an importance beyond calculation. A lavish nature, tropical climate, and prolific soil have rendered their possession valuable. They will be the cause of contention and competition in the future.

Is it not essential that we should be vigilant as to our true interests at this point? The British jack is there, barring the entrance to this route, and the roar of the old lion can be heard now on the coast of Venezuela and in little Nicaragua. Shall we sit idly by while the Monroe doctrine is assailed and our ramparts are being taken? Great Britain already holds the keys to navigation in the West Indies. She owns Jamaica—Cromwell wrested it from the Spaniards in 1655—and Kingston is the base of operations of the British West India fleet. It lies but ninety miles from Cuba and a short distance from San Domingo, supervising, more than we imagine, our coast trade. Britain's flag floats over the Caman islands, Trinidad, St. Vincent, the Barbadoes, St. Lucia and the Bahamas, as well as the eastern coast of Yucatan and British Honduras, all strongly fortified. Spain controls Cuba and Porto Rico, both of which are deemed of sufficient importance to warrant that poverty-stricken country to go to war for their maintenance and retention.

In the space of this response I cannot touch upon the importance of Cuba to the United States, but may be pardoned for expressing the hope that, during the life of this generation, it may, as it should, become a part of our own country. France owns the islands of Guadaloupe and Martinique, lying well up toward Mona Passage, but San Domingo rises above them all with special advantages and a special prominence. Had President Grant's fervent wish been granted, our flag to-day would wave over the island; and, from the folds of its stars and stripes dedicated to liberty and union, would float out over the gulf and sea, a spirit of patriotism tempering the entire archipelago. San Domingo was the first island of the Western Hemisphere colonized by Europeans. Near it was born Alexander Hamilton, whose ashes still rule us from their urn, and here Christopher Columbus was buried in accordance with his own expressed desire.

Should it have been accepted when tendered? Then how much more important, in the light of the present day, is it that we accept the Hawaiian islands, situated with reference to our own country as advantageously in the Pacific as San Domingo is at the Gulf. Would there be any doubt as to the wisdom of this country extending its jurisdiction over the Bermudas in the Atlantic, if they were offered to us as freely as were Domingo and the Sandwich Islands? The faintest encouragement would have been sufficient for Great Britain to encircle these islands. And this generation owes it to those that follow to lessen the possibilities of war, by taking into the national union these naval outposts in both oceans.

It was asserted a hundred years ago, by students of European history, that, if America should become free, she would, one day, give the law to Europe. She would take away her islands and her colonies. She would seize the Antilles. She would acquire Mexico and possess herself of Chili and Brazil. How much of this prophecy should be realized in this day and age of advancing civilization?

A hundred years ago, it was predicted of our nation, that it would, some day, stretch its arms upon the two oceans and direct the vessels from one to the other by an artificial route, through Lake Nicaragua, that would change the course of the commercial world and the face of empires. Shall we justify the prophecies of these seers of old, and while rigidly adhering to the doctrine emphasized by Monroe and maintained with more or less exactness by each of his successors, apply it as firmly to other nations as we have rigidly observed it ourselves.

In this hour of territorial acquisition and trade conquest, may we not well pause and consider the earnest and heartfelt desire of our greatest military captain and one of our best Presidents, in honor of whose birthday we are assembled, and take up the work of closer political relationship with the republic of San Domingo at the South, and Hawaii, the young republic of the West, standing like sentinels on guard over the gateway from the Atlantic, the Pacific and the Tropic sea, and mindful of the foresight, wisdom and patriotism breathed out of his loyal soul, as he passed from earth to heaven, pray the divine hand to part the cloud obscuring our vision, that we may catch again his lofty spirit, and see by his clear light the way of true greatness for our country and our flag.

"DOCTORS, LAWYERS, PREACHERS, BUSINESS MEN."

Response by Joseph B. Connell, B. S., LL. B., M. D., Kansas City, Mo., at banquet of Michigan University Alumni at Kansas City, Mo., April, 1896.

I believe with De Tocqueville who said, "There are no professions in America, everything is an art or a trade." There being no large leisure class here, the bread and butter problem enters into every calling, and the professions deal largely in commodities, which are regulated by the law of supply and demand. Even religion is no exception, and we realize that salvation is no longer free for you and me, but costs money. We speak no longer of a doctor's or a lawyer's practice, but of his business; nor of the size of a preacher's congregation, but of his salary. The fact is, competition in the professions, together with the growth of popular intelligence, are working revolutions in professional aims and methods and are demanding of each that it render the "quid pro quo" in genuine equivalent for the professional fee. Why, popular intelligence is in the very air in America. It is said we breathe 18 to 20 times a minute where the Englishman breathes 15 to 18 times; and from this increased oxidation, there arises increased cerebration which, aided by free schools, the press, and public discussion, is elevating popular intelligence so high that the people have lost their reverence for authority. They demand the causes and the reasons, and subject every idea to the alembic of their own experience. The people are running this government—not the politicians. The pews and not the preachers are running the pulpit. Popular opinion is behind the law. And the people are largely running the medical profession, though we have them at a disadvantage—when they are down. It is remarkable how the per-

sonnel of the professions has changed within the memory
of those now living.   Why, even I can remember the old-
fashioned preacher as a long, solemn, ominous, individual,
full of dismal forebodings—when in order to be religious
one had to become bilious.   Such a man does not succeed
to-day!   My old idea of a doctor was similar—a cross between a preacher and an undertaker, who entered the sick
room, mysterious and profound.   He is not popular to-
day!   The frontier lawyer is described by Lincoln.   "He
mounted the rostrum, threw back his head, 'shined' his eyes,
opened his mouth, and left the consequences to God!"
Such a man is not popular to-day!   The demand is not for
that class of lawyers portrayed in Warren's Ten Thousand
a Year, as the great BBB's—Bluffers of courts, browbeaters
of witnesses, and bulldozers of juries.   Not for those who
so far forget themselves as to become mere vials of vitriol
to be hurled at an antagonist—mere missiles of anger and
revenge.   The demand is not for a blackmailer, but for a
business lawyer, one who is firm, yet just; one who keeps
us out of litigation, for the good all around office man.   I
admit the other genius still flourishes somewhat in country
towns, but the good office man gets the best class of business and makes the most money.   So the demand is not
for the religion of fear, but of love, and we are willing to
pay for it.   So the demand is not for the cure of disease by
black cat skins, or potatoes in the pocket, or the left hind
foot of a rabbit killed in the dark of the moon.   The people
demand the rational scientific medicine, which seeks the
cause of disease and helps nature in its cure.   Why are law
and medicine specializing?   It is a business principle, according to the law of division of labor—each becoming pro-
ficient along certain exclusive lines.   It narrows one down
to a sharper cutting edge.

Now, in medicine we have a certain unwritten code of
ethics which says "no one shall advertise but me."   And if
a doctor gets a puff—all the rest, like anarchists, are jealous

and pull him down for taking an unfair advantage. But we can't find fault with specialism, for it is legitimate advertising—advertising by inference, and it pays. The only difference between legal and medical specialism is that the lawyer must earn his specialty, while in medicine it can be adopted.

Why are contingent fees growing in size and frequency? And why are private hospitals becoming essential? It is a plain business principle. Capital is becoming an essential to the professions. But you say is not medicine a charitable profession? Look at the colleges and free hospitals and dispensaries for the poor. Does not the doctor give his services gratis—from pure philanthropy? Not exactly. He reminds me of the dialogue between father and daughter. "Daughter, is not that young man a member of the coal combine? Yes, sir. Isn't he a member of the gas company? Yes, sir. Well, my daughter, I am afraid his attentions to you are not entirely disinterested." So with the doctors. Competition forces them to keep before the people, and their charity services are as bread cast upon the waters, which may return to them after many days in increased experience, a better class of patients and better pay.

Now, in my judgment, strange as it may seem, the same essentials to success exist in all the professions—address, policy, hard work, money, influence, character. The differences between professional men are not causes, but effects of different kinds of work. Bacon says, "Speaking maketh a ready man, reading maketh a full man, writing maketh an exact man;" and this is the whole thing in a nutshell. Doctors are quiet, careful, studious, scientific. Preachers are literary, persuasive, rhetorical. Lawyers are ready, fluent, logical, diplomatic.

It is said the average United States Senator has the best disciplined mind in America. Why? Because he has generally been a lawyer, and his legal and political battles, his

many attritions have developed a wonderful mental strength
and equipoise, together with a superlative cheek, which is
the admiration and the envy of the civilized world?

Now, I should be sorry to feel that there was nothing
but money in the professions. That the doctor relieved
suffering at so much a pain. That the preacher paved the
way to heaven at so much per pavement. Or that the wit
of the orator was so much a haw haw! For over and above
it all, the professions are the only beacon lights which poor,
frail humanity has to guide and guard; and oftentimes they
shed a radiance as immeasurable in money as the radiance
of the stars!

Now, financially, no profession is a gold mine. If
money is your object—like the boys' three roads to town—
whichever road you take, you wish you had took t'other.
All are overestimated. And most of us, when expenses are
paid, could cry with Wolsey, "My robe and my integrity
to heaven are all I dare now call mine own!"

But I hold, as a business proposition, that any class or
calling stands with the people, in proportion to the prompti-
tude with which it pays its debts.

Lawyers and preachers, pay your debts! Keep your
credit, like Caesar's wife, above suspicion. Now some
preachers—not all—are apt to saddle their bills on to the
trustees, or to mentally give a mortgage on their mansion
in the skies. Some lawyers—not all—are apt to say, "Let
my creditors wait! Who dare sue a lawyer?"

Now, in other respects I grant you, the doctor is a poor
business man. He has no time for himself. About the
time he begins to think about his own investments, somebody's baby gets the colic and away goes the doctor, and
away goes his plans—till baby has recovered, and then away
has gone his opportunity. If you want to gull somebody,
if you want to coax money out of somebody, go and flatter
some fool doctor, and you'll get your money! Hasn't time
to investigate! But the doctor pays his bills best of all.

Why? Is it that he makes more money? Not a bit. Is he a good collector? He is a poor collector? More honest? Hardly. It is because his income is more regular. Now, in this respect, I'd rather sell peanuts than pianos. Because you sell peanuts every day and the season's all the year around! So I'd rather practise medicine every day, and have my income from month to month so as to meet my obligations as they arise, than to preach or practise law and have my income at some salary day, or some term of court, and nothing hardly the rest of the year. I'd feel better, stand better, work better, develop better, pay better. Speed the day when in all professions chicanery shall cease, and when all shall be so conducted on business principles that they can look every man in the face and grow in public patronage and esteem!

But in another respct the doctor has the advantage over the lawyer. He pays the debt of nature more gracefully. Why? In religious opinion most lawyers are agnostics. Why? It is an effect and not a cause. With the lawyer life is spent unraveling conflicting human testimony. He learns that no two men can see or hear or tell the same fact the same way; that nothing is reliable. That the best witnesses are biased or have faulty perception or memory. One of our highest courts' recently decided a man was dead. Several saw him drown. The witnesses so swore. The court ignored any other theory. The jury so believed and it was so decided. No doubt about it. He was dead and paid for. And now the man appears and says it isn't true!

Nothing reliable! And hence he comes to the conclusion that Divine revelation written by human pen, is unreliable, and he cries, with Ingersoll, "I am an agnostic, I don't know!"

Most doctors are materialists. Why? A student of medicine is a student of nature. He knows a little of botany and geology and anatomy, a little of Fauna and Flora, of field and forest and stream. He can "go forth into the open sky and list to Nature and her teachings." Better than the Duke in "As You Like It," can he "find tongues in trees, books in the running brooks, sermons in stones and good in everything." He looks through the body with the Roentgen ray. He sees it disintegrate under the knife and under the forces of Nature. He studies its histological structure under the miscroscope, and he says this is all of man, the end is here and now. Man is but an aggregation of cells with separate functions—differentiated protoplasm. He dies, and is chemically broken up into carbonic acid, water, ammonia, and the earthy salts, and is absorbed by the earth and air and tree and flower, and joins the eternal cycle of life and death through all the ages that shall come and go! And that is all there is of it. No present but of the flesh, no future but of earth and sky! And from this belief there arises a quiet satisfaction with the problem of life, a broader conception of Nature and the universe, an inspiration broader than creed—this "looking through Nature, up to Nature's God!"

"THE LEGAL PROFESSION."

Response by Frank T. Lodge, of Detroit, Mich., at the annual banquet of the Michigan College of Medicine and Surgery, at the Wayne Hotel, Detroit, Mich., March 6, 1895.

Mr. Toastmaster, Ladies and Gentlemen:

If your toastmaster were still a member of the Health Board of Detroit (which, fortunately for the health and hopes of the community, he is not), I might say that, with this introduction I had been duly placarded, and, at the conclusion of this speech, I would be put into the strictest quarantine. I have been wondering, as I sat here, why I was chosen to respond to this toast. Frequenters of banquets and connoisseurs of after-dinner oratory are aware that the chief requisite of most of those who speak on

occasions like this, seems to be their complete ignorance of
the subject assigned to them.   Like Mark Twain, in his
famous Essay on Milk, they talk about everything else in
the world but their subject, and, apparently, know nothing
about that.   In view of this well-known practice upon banquet occasions, I am surprised that I, a lawyer, living and
working in the very atmosphere of the law, and supposed
to know all about it, should be called upon to display my
ignorance of it by responding to it as a toast.

Upon second thought, however, the harrowing suspicion
forces itself upon my mind that your committee who assigned me this subject and your toastmaster who has called
me up, knew their business better than I thought they did.
A certain practitioner at our bar used frequently to be
called "Old Necessity," because it has passed into a proverb
that "Necessity knows no law."   Perhaps I am the "Old
Necessity" of this glittering and splendid program.   Perhaps the very reason I was asked to represent the legal
profession this evening is because of the clearly defined
impression in the minds of the committee that I know so
little of the subject that it may safely be entrusted to me.

I can therefore assure you, Mr. Toastmaster, that the
topic has already become a painful one to me, by reason of
the uncertainty in which my real relation to it is involved;
and, were it not for the "reasonable doubt" of which the
law gives every criminal,—even a lawyer,—the benefit, I
would feel unable to proceed.   Fortified, however, by the
fact that the law presumes me to be guilty of knowledge,
at least until this speech shall have proven me innocent, I
shall persevere to the bitter end.

I have no doubt that scores of physicians firmly believe
that the legal profession is an invention of the Devil, especially devised by "His Black Majesty" for the torture of
gentlemen of their cloth, so that, by driving them to the
brink of suicide or the unctuous profanity which can fall so

smoothly from their lips, he may thereby largely recruit his ranks from the wielders of the scalpel and lancet.

And who that has seen the physician after first testifying on oath that he is a competent expert, finally tangled up in inextricable labyrinths, tied into Gordian knots by innocent-appearing, but dangerous cross-examination, and then dismissed, with flushed face and angry heart, half dead with rage and mortification, who, I say, can blame such a physician if he lacks a warm affection for the profession which has made him appear so ridiculous.

To be sure, the physician's turn comes sooner or later. Lawyers are no more exempt from the common heritage of ills that belong to all flesh than are other mortals, and the lawyer must, perforce, call in the physician once in a while. When the physician gets through with him, the account between them is more than evened up, except that, because of his liberal donations during life to church and charity, the lawyer's estate never seems to be large enough to defray the expenses of his last illness, including, of course, the inevitable "doctor's bill."

It is true, the physician sometimes makes a slip, and cures the lawyer, even to his own undoing. I remember an instance of a physician who presented his bill for professional services to a lawyer, who had recently recovered from a serious illness. The lawyer pleaded inability to pay, claiming to have used all his money in meeting an insurance assessment. "Are you insured?" asked the physician with a startled air. "Yes," said the lawyer, "and, in case of my death, the proceeds of the insurance are to be first applied to paying the expense of my last illness." "Humph," said the physician reflectively, "I wish I had known that sooner. I think I would have gotten my money.

But, joking aside, I am glad to respond to this toast to-night. I am glad to see two liberal professions, like yours and mine, Mr. Toastmaster, joining hands in their lighter, as they so frequently do in their more serious, moments. I am glad that we may, for a brief season, step aside from the rush and bustle, to catch our breath; that we may, to-night, readjust our measurements and take anew our bearings, looking upward at the Pole Star of Truth that our course may be straighter and steadier because of this observation.

The legal profession is one of the so-called learned and liberal professions. This means that its exponents should bring to the exercise of their calling, higher qualities of head and heart than are demanded in the ordinary walks of life. It is the lawyer's high mission to bring to light, and to firmly establish, the very truth.

In every case he tries, the ideal lawyer seeks "The truth, the whole truth and nothing but the truth," no matter how darkly it may be obscured by the base designs of wicked men. It is for this purpose that law courts are established, and juries of laymen, from the very vicinage, are called; and all the technical rules and hair-splitting distinctions of the law, all the complicated machinery of Justice, have but the single end and aim of ascertaining and establishing the truth. Of this vast, complicated mechanism the lawyer is the engineer. He sets the wheels in motion. He directs and regulates the whole. And as the rights of man attach to everything in the known world, and as those rights are frequently in dispute, it results that the lawyer deals with the facts of every science and pursuit.

To-day he is in a horse case, and must know all the details of ring-bone, spavin, heaves and broken wind; to-morrow he must discuss the recondite principles of mechanics, and the next day, perhaps, try to recover the wages of a servant girl. The lawyer probes the highest and lowest springs of human action. It is his task to deal with the intangible essence of the mind and soul, to exactly weigh impenetrable motives, to carefully define the delicate balance of the brain, marking, without mistake, just where right reason leaves off and insanity begins. Alone, unaided, ofttimes without even the feeble glimmer of a single star, he must explore the dark, mysterious, unknown and unknowable realm of Circumstantial Evidence. Through it, he must thread his way, along a devious path that is full of the wraiths of Justice gone astray, of black-hearted guilt triumphantly acquitted and innocence sent to its grave in grief and shame. In a pathway full of pitfalls, he must make no misstep, for on his skill hang property, reputation, yea, even life itself.

Is it not small wonder, then, that he should often need the friendly aid of the physician's skill? Where so many cases of crime, reputation and property rights depend so largely upon the most wonderful of all mysteries, the human body and its varied pathology, is it a matter of surprise that the earnest lawyer should make lavish drafts upon the skill and learning of the physician?

Many cases of crime could never be cleared up without the testimony of expert physicians, who, although they may know nothing about the facts of the particular case, yet from the uniform operation of natural laws, with which they are well acquainted, can testify as to what probably occurred in the case with as much certainty as if they had been personally present as eye witnesses. It is for this reason that the whole subject of expert testimony has been admitted into the law, and expert physicians are now permitted to testify as such, not that they may show off their skill and learning, not that they may floor lawyer, judge and jury with the sesquipedalian jargon of their technical terms, but that they may "make light the dark places," and "make plain that which was hid." The physician then becomes a co-worker with the lawyer, a ministering priest with him in the snow-white Temple of Truth. His best and highest efforts should be freely laid as a fragrant offering

upon her holy altar. Advocate of neither side, foe to
neither, his sole desire should be to make plain the truth,
let the result be what it may, and let him beware lest he
trail his holy calling in the dust.

I have but one word of advice to offer to the young
gentlemen and ladies of the graduating class who may,
perhaps very soon, be called upon to help the lawyer in the
courts as expert witnesses: First, know thoroughly what
you are called to testifiy about, and then tell it simply and
plainly in the queen's pure English, free from the slightest
suspicion of Latin. Shun the example of a recent graduate, who testified in an assault and battery case, that he
found the plaintiff suffering from a severe contusion of the
integuments under the left orbit, with great extravasation of
blood and ecchymosis in the surrounding cellular tissue,
which was in a tumefied state, together with considerable
abrasion of the cuticle. "My gracious!" exclaimed the
judge, "was it as bad as that? I thought his only damage
was a black eye." "Why, so it was," said the witness, "that
is what I meant." "Then," roared the judge, "why in thun-
der didn't you say so?"

Do not be afraid of being too simple and plain in your
explanations. It is astonishing what queer ideas jurors
get, and upon what wild tangents their verdicts sometimes
go off. The famous Scotch verdict, "Not guilty, but he'd
better never do it again," is no overdrawn burlesque of
some verdicts which are still actually rendered.

I remember hearing Mr. Don M. Dickinson, in this
very room, on a similar occasion, tell the following incident
of his early practice: One of his first cases was against a
railroad company for damages because of his client's having been violently thrown against the back of a car seat,
striking across his stomach, and, as he claimed, totally dis-
abling him. In the course of his preparation of the case,
Mr. Dickinson concluded that he would look up a little

expert testimony, so he went to his client's family physician, who said that the man was permanently disabled, and gave his reasons for his opinion. It, of course, pleased Mr. Dickinson to learn that his client was permanently disabled, but he concluded to reinforce his opinion with that of another physician; so that he went to see another—and just here is where he made a mistake. He told Physician No. 2 what Physician No. 1 had said, and gave his reasons for it. Physician No. 2 said that the opinion of Physician No. 1 was arrant nonsense. Of course the man was not permanently disabled, and he gave his reasons for his opinion. Somewhat crestfallen and chagrined to find that his client was not so badly damaged as he had hoped, Mr. Dickinson consulted Physician No. 3 and told him the opinion of Physician No. 2 and his reasons for that opinion. Physician No. 3 was astonished and shocked to learn that such an idiotic opinion had been given by anyone claiming to be a physician, and said that such a man was a disgrace to their honorable profession. Of course the man was permanently disabled, and he gave his reasons for thinking so. Thus reinforced, and with his spirits cheered by the thought of his client's permanent disability, Mr. Dickinson went into the trial of the case. There were one lawyer and three doctors on one side, and one lawyer and four doctors on the other.

The family physician was sworn, and, in the course of his cross-examination by the attorney for the defendant, he was asked what treatment he gave to promote the peristaltic action of the bowels. Among other questions, he was asked, "Did the patient knead his bowels?" and answered it in the affirmative. At the conclusion of the testimony, the arguments and judge's charge, the jury retired and promptly returned with a verdict for Mr. Dickinson's client. After the jury were discharged, Mr. Dickinson shook hands with them and thanked them for the verdict. He finally came to Michael Joy, who, in his day, was a famous character around the Court House, frequently serving on juries. "Well, Mr. Joy," said Mr. Dickinson, "I am very much obliged for your verdict. By the way, what do you think of the expert testimony?" "Aye, ixpert tistimony," answered Mr. Joy, "fwhat's that?" "Why," said Mr. Dickinson, "the testimony of the doctors." "Oh, the dochtors!" exclaimed Mr. Joy, with a grin, "the dochtors! Do a man nade his bowels? Do a man nade his bowels? Dom the dochtors! say I. Let's sock it to the railroads!"

I would not have you think, Mr. Toastmaster, that this eulogy of my profession is a fair and faithful picture of every lawyer in it, for it is not. To our common shame, be it said, that there is empiricism and shallow pretense in both law and medicine, as well as in every other walk of life. To our common shame, be it said, that there are shysters as well as charlatans, pettifoggers as well as quacks. I have been talking of what should be, not what always actually is. But it is only by the contemplation of the lofty ideal that we can ever hope to lift the actual up into its purer ether, and it has been with the sincere hope that you and I, Mr. Toastmaster, and all of us, may bathe our spirits in the lofty ideal and go hence cheered and refreshed with a holy determination to elevate and purify our respective callings, that I have ventured to bring before your vision a few of its many beauties.

All hail, then, to the Legal Profession! We share the highest hopes and holiest emotions of your own sister calling. We are brothers and coadjutors in our search for the white light of Truth, and so long as a wrong remains to be righted, so long as guilt remains unpunished and innocence bows its head in shame, just so long will the professions of law and medicine join hands and hearts and journey forth like knights of old, as champions of the Right.

"THE LAWYER."

Response by H. H. Wilson, of Lincoln, Neb., at a reunion of the Union
Literary Society of the University of Nebraska, June, 1883.

Ladies and Gentlemen:

A lawyer is generally understood to be one who will
talk with equal eloquence on either side of any question—
for a valuable consideration. And the eloquence usually
bears some proportion to the amount of the consideration.

It was, I believe, Lord Brougham who said that the
lawyer should know no God but his client; and it will be
generally conceded, I think, that few of them ever transgress
by pushing their inquiries any further.

Of all classes of the community, perhaps the lawyers
are the most peaceable, which is due, no doubt, to the fact
that their time is so fully occupied in conducting the quarrels of others. It would, however, be a great mistake to
infer from their quiet nature that they are wanting in the
elements of fortitude and bravery. An Irish advocate once
went so far as to challenge his opponent to mortal combat
and fixed the place of meeting "in the Phoenix Park, adja-
cent unto the City of Dublin, and in that part of it entitled
'The Fifteen Acres,' be the same more or less."

The natural history of the lawyer presents many points
of interest. It would seem that the lawyer is a result of
Darwin's Development of the Species. It is quite certain
that he must have had his origin since the flood, for careful
examination fails to show any mention of him in the bill
of lading of that memorable cargo.

Some antiquarians claim to have found fossil remains of
the antediluvian lawyer, but either these worthy gentlemen
have been misled, or else the lawyer was not registered on
that trip, perhaps because he traveled on a pass.

The proper classification of the lawyer, no less than his
origin, has given rise to much controversy. M. De Tocqueville seems to regard him as a cross between the aristocrat

of England and the revolutionist of France, while Bentham declares that he is not an independent being at all, but a parasite subsisting on the vitality of others.

Whatever difference of opinion may exist as to the origin and proper classification of the lawyer, there can be none as to the location and extent of his habitat.

Specimens may be found in every civilized country except in the Island of Utopia, and some have even doubted the accuracy of Sir Thomas' history because he states positively that no lawyers are to be found on that island.

There is a tradition that Webster once said of lawyers that there is always room at the top, but it may well be doubted whether he ever made so general a statement and one so derogatory to his chosen profession, although doubtless many do have rooms to rent in their upper story.

Of late years our fair sisters have begun to doubt our ability to conduct their quarrels in a truly feminine spirit and have demanded a place by our side.

We welcome them to the forum of ennobling strife and to share with us the rewards of bloodless victories.

And hereafter when we speak of our honored profession we must be understood to embrace our sisters-in-law.

"A DOCTOR'S IMPRESSION CONCERNING LAWYERS."

At the first annual banquet of the Law Students' Association of Chicago, in representing the Kent College of Law, the following remarks were made by Dr. G. Frank Lydston, one of the lecturers in said college, upon the above topic.

Mr. Symposiarch, Ladies and Gentlemen: It requires some assurance to enable one to rise to his feet and attempt to speak in the presence of such accomplished orators as are present this evening, and while listening to those who have already spoken, I have resolved to escape as easily as I can by sticking very closely to my text. Inasmuch as the text was not taken from the Bible, this will be comparatively

easy for me to do.   It may seem peculiar to some of you
that a doctor should be called upon to respond in behalf of
a Law School.   I can assure you, however, that it is not because Kent is a young school and needs medical care.   It
had its teeth cut some time since, and has passed through
all of its infantile complaints successfully.   It has no ail-
ments now, except growing pains, and we do not wish these
to be relieved.

While listening to the remarks of the preceding speaker,
who so ably represents the Chicago College of Law, I ex-
perienced a pang of keen regret that I had not brought
with me a laurel wreath for Kent College.   But a ready-
made wreath would not do, and the manufacturer from
whom I ordered a custom-made one, was out of material
before he got half way round the brow of Kent.   We do
not need a halo, but are willing to be in fashion, so that, in
case the Chicago College has a second-hand halo, that it
does not need for its clients, we will wear it for harmony's
sake.   The fact is, I was selected because the legal members
of the faculty are so modest that they cannot bear to hear
themselves talk—a frequent complaint among law teachers,
but one which is in no danger of becoming epidemic among
law students.   Another excellent excuse for my being on
the same planet with such distinguished legal lights as I
see about this festive board, is that I am a sort of a lawyer
myself.   I am a lawyer in something the same remote fashion that a certain Kentuckian was a colonel.   He said that
he was a colonel by marriage, his wife's first husband having been killed at Gettysburg.   I am a lawyer, not by marriage, for my wife's relations were people of the highest respectability, but by adoption.   I feel under the deepest obligations for the opportunity of being with you this evening.
It is seldom that I have a chance to study the lawyer
in his lair—at the banquet table.   It is, indeed, a blessed
privilege to meet so many kinds of lawyers as are present
to-night.   I see about me about all the varieties of the

genus lawyer. Judges, who run law dispensaries, where a dram of justice is so skillfully mixed with a barrel of law, that the unwary layman is fain to take his medicine without flinching. The law and the lady—the female lawyer, against whom I shall enter a replevin suit to-morrow—cause,—one lost heart. Law professors who toil not neither do they spin, but make a business of professing. Patent lawyers, so called, I presume, because, like a country newspaper, they have patent insides—an attribute which is patent enough to one who has ever watched them irrigating or feeding the inner man. Real estate lawyers, who hold mortgages on cemeteries and fifteen-story buildings. Divorce lawyers, who act equally well as attorney, complainant or defendant, but would shine with effulgent brilliancy as co-respondent. Corporation lawyers, whose corporations are sometimes large, but often no larger than common mortals with good appetites. Last, but not least, that practical humanitarian, the criminal lawyer, whose clients are all angels in due time, and who could have proven an alibi for the devil himself, in that famous affair in the Garden of Eden. Then there is the coming lawyer, who is largely present in embryo this evening as the student of law.

According to my observation, lawyers and doctors are divided into classes, very much as a certain market man in Fulton market, in New York, divided his eggs. He had a rival who made a specialty of Jersey eggs, and was making a howling success. Nothing daunted, our friend placed some baskets of eggs outside his door and labeled them as follows:

Strictly fresh eggs 30cts per dozen.
Fresh eggs   -   25cts a dozen.
Eggs   20cts.
Jersey eggs   15cts.

There may be Jersey eggs in the legal profession, but they are certainly not here to-night.

The profession of law has many advantages over that

of medicine. No doctor wes ever known to get himself
patented. He may consider himself a good thing, but he
dare not push it along. The ethics of the profession forbid
it. We are highly moral people, and consequently there are
no criminal doctors. Even our novelists are compelled to
go outside of the medical profession to find their villains.
Dr. Jekyll must become Mr. Hyde (who was probably a
lawyer), in order to be interesting. We have no divorce
doctors because we are too familiar with both sides of such
cases. We have lady doctors, but I object to them as a
temptation to overdosing, just as I am opposed to lady
lawyers as tempting one to perpetually litigate. Corporations have no use for doctors, because when a man falls
off a ten-story building and sits down good and hard upon
his antipodes, or in that immediate vicinity—we say that he
has spinal concussion, and the poor fallen man gets big
damages. You see we doctors are practical, moralistic
philanthropists, and sympathize deeply with poor fallen
men. It is no wonder that we are all experts until you fellows get after us. We have no real estate doctors, because
we never get rich enough to own real estate. Our interest in
all buildings is largely theoretical, and we pay very dearly
for it, when the landlord is sharp enough to make us. As
for the base slander that we have any interest in cemeteries,
save as places for cold storage, it is unworthy of grave consideration. Indeed, I may say that it is a monumental lie.
That we are in cahoots with the undertaker is also a vile
calumny. We recognize the undertaker as belonging to a
distinct profession, a sort of post-medical profession, as it
were. We never associate with them, but send our office
boy to collect our commission. He will henceforth be our
enemy, for I understand that he has adopted a new name,
and now calls himself a "mortician." The term, to be sure,
is more lucid than the old one, and it is certainly much
more euphonious, but by all the gods it rhymes with physician too prettily to suit me. Taken all in all, you lawyers

have the best or it. I have noticed, however, that the two professions resemble each other in many respects. Doctors never attend funerals, and lawyers give away their tickets for executions. Neither the doctor nor the lawyer likes to be caught red-handed, with the dead sheep over his shoulder. Both are willing to forego the pleasure of being in at the death, but it is surprising to note the equanimity and unanimity of purpose with which they bob up serenly and greet each other in a probate court. You have all heard that old chestnut about the Irishman, who, upon seeing the epitaph which read, "Here lies the body of John Smith, a lawyer and an honest man," exclaimed "Be jabbers, Mike, they do be's afther puttin' two min in wan grave." I thought that story was real funny, and told it to one of my lawyer friends, who reciprocated by telling me this little fable— probably from Aesop or Blackstone, or the Baron Munchausen, or some other high legal authority. "Once upon a time a good medical man was watching a funeral procession, and pondering awhile on the 'much and goodly game which he betimes had brought to pot,' a dog, who was also watching the funeral train, said to him, Say doc, ain't it funny? When I bury a bone I do it so that I may dig it up again and pick it by and by, while you bury your stuff for keeps.' The doctor was a truthful, Godly man, and made reply, 'Never mind, doggie, don't you fret, the bones I bury are well picked before I bury them.'"

But, seriously, ladies and gentlemen, I esteem it a great privilege to be associated—no matter how remotely, with the legal profession. The profession of law is more aptly termed a learned profession than either medicine or the ministry. It is in the profession of law that the man of broad culture and scholarly attainments receives his highest appreciation. My own profession is so tainted with modern so-called specialism, that the veriest dunce may achieve public notoriety and at least financial success. Too often does he receive the adulation of the body medical. The accomplished, scholarly, cultured physician is in danger of becoming lost in the race for wealth. It is easier to pander to a simple-minded public by commercial shrewdness than to win appreciation of scholarly attainments by solid merit. So much the worse for medicine. Thank heaven that so many mistakes are hidden by good old mother earth. It is not surprising that the lawyer has so little respect for the medical expert. Was it not a lawyer who divided witnesses into liars, d—d liars and medical experts? Fortunately the so-called expert is not always a fair criterion of the intelligence and honesty of the medical profession.

The personnel of the professional man has greatly changed for the better within a few decades. Time was when the legal profession was supposed to be represented by a seedy-looking individual, with a lurid nose and a breath which suggested the possibility of spontaneous combustion. This individual had a little den somewhere in town, the furniture of which consisted of much dirt and a few law books. Notwithstanding this fact, his admiring neighbors said he could try a case better when he was drunk than some men could when sober. This apostle of the law is now a relic of the past. The lawyer of to-day must be a clean, sober, cultured gentleman, or a charming woman, or he or she may not rise above the level of a shyster. It is no longer considered unprofessional to have a clean office and a decent library. The old-time squire has been relegated to the valley of dead lumber, along with that good, old besotted doctor, who was so awfully good for children when he was sober, and who in all his life never rose above the dignity of "Doc"—the most opprobrious epithet ever applied to a medical man.

In the profession of law, talent and scholarly attainments soon find their level in these modern days. I have noticed, too, that there is an esprit du corps among lawyers which is sadly lacking among doctors. I have observed that most lawyers have much that is good to say of each other. When a man distinguishes himself in law, his brethren vie with each other in doing him honor. In medicine, the great man's achievements are brilliant in inverse proportion to his proximity to those who comment upon them. There is usually a qualifying clause, a sort of damning with faint praise. This is not true of the profession of law. It would be well if the sentiment of personal honor, which every lawyer worthy of the name, cherishes so highly, could permeate every profession.

Members of the bar, I congratulate you upon your affiliation with so broad and learned a profession. Students of the law, I congratulate you upon your prospective membership in a profession in which all of the attributes of good fellowship are combined with the highest appreciation of all the good which you can possibly accomplish. What greater incentive can be offered you, for real, earnest and conscientious work? It should be a consolation to you in your hours of studious toil, to feel that your light need never be put under a bushel, that your professional work is sure to count,—not only upon the public upon which you depend for a livelihood, but better still, with the members of your own profession.

"WAMPUM, OR THE FREE COINAGE OF CLAMS."

Response by Joseph C. Hendrix, of New York City, to toast "Wampum," at dinner of New England Society of Brooklyn, N. Y., Dec. 21, 1894.

Some one has described Peter as the shortest man mentioned in the Bible, because he said: "Gold and silver have I none," and surely no one could be shorter than that. The North American Indian was no better off than Peter in his gold reserve or silver supply; but he managed to get along with the Quahog clam. That was the money substance out of which he made the wampum, and the shell-heaps scattered over this island are mute monuments to an industry which was blasted by the demonetization of the hard-shell clam. Wampum was a good money in the Indian civilization. It was the product of human labor, as difficult and tedious as the labor of the gold miner of to-day.

It had intrinsic value, for it was redeemable in anything the Indian had to give, from his skill in the chase to his squaw. It took time, patience, endurance and skill to make a thing of beauty out of a clam, even in the eyes of an Indian, but when the squaws and the old men had ground down the tough end of the shell to the size of a wheat straw, and had bored it with a sliver of flint, and strung it upon a thew of deerskin, and tested its smoothness on the nose, they had an article which had as much power over an Indian mind as a grain of gold to-day has over us. There were two kinds of wampum. The blue and the white. The Montauks to this day know that there is a difference between the two. The blue came from our clam. The white, which was the product of the periwinkle, did not need so much labor to fit it for use as wampum, and it was cheaper. The blue was the gold; the white was the silver. One blue bead was worth two white ones. The Indians did not try to keep up any parity of the beads. They let each kind go for just what it was worth. The Puritans used to restring the beads and keep the blue ones. Then the Indians strung their scalps.

Why was wampum good money in its time? The supply was limited. It took a day to make four or five beads. It was in itself a thing of value to the Indian for ornament. It was easily carried about from place to place. It was practically indestructible. It was always alike. It was divisible. The value attaching to it did not vary. It was not easily counterfeited. So it was that it became the money of the colonists; a legal tender in Massachusetts, and the tool of the primitive commerce of this continent. The Puritan took it for fire water, and gave it back for furs. Long Island was the great mint for this pastoral coinage. It was called the "mine of the New Netherland." The Indian walked the beach at Rockaway, dug his toes in the sand, turned up a clam, and after swallowing the contents carried the shells to the mint. Gold and silver at the mouth of a mine obtain their chief value from the labor it takes to get the metals, wampum was the refinement by labor of a money substance free to all. The redemption of wampum was perfect. To the Indian it was a seal to treaties, an amulet in danger, an affidavit, small change, a savings bank, a wedding ring and a dress suit. To this day the belt of wampum is the storehouse of Indian treasure. In the Six Nations, when a big chief made an assertion in council, he laid down a belt of wampum, as though to say "money talks." The Iroquois sent a belt of it to the King of England, when they asked his protection. William Penn got a strip when he made his treaty. The Indians braided rude pictures into it, which recorded great events. They talked their ideas into it, as we do into a phonograph. They sent messages in it. White beads between a row of dark ones represented a path of peace, as though to say, "Big chief no longer got Congress on his hands." A string of dark beads was a message of war, or of the death of a chief, and a string of white beads rolled in mud was equivalent to saying that there was crape on the door of Tammany Hall. So you see that it was a combined postoffice, telegraph, telephone, phonograph and newspaper.

The Iroquois had a keeper of wampum—a sort of secretary of the treasury, without the task of keeping nine different kinds of money on a parity. This old Indian financier had simple and correct principles. No one could persuade him to issue birchbark promises to pay, and to delude himself with the belief that he could thus create money. He certainly would have called them a debt, and would have paid them off as fast as he could. Nor can we imagine him trying to sustain the value of the white wampum after the Puritans started in to make it out of oyster shells by ma-

chinery. Nor would he have bought it, not needing it, and
have issued against it his promises to pay in good wampum
as fast and as often as they were presented.

It was said that wampum was so cunningly made that
neither Jew nor Devil could counterfeit it. Nevertheless,
a Connecticut Yankee rigged up a machine that so dis-
turbed the market value of the beads that in a short time
the Long Island mints were closed to the free coinage of
clams. Wampum was demonetized through counterfeiting,
over-production and imitation; but when this occurred the
gentle Puritan didn't have enough of it left to supply the
museums. The Indian had parted with his lands and his
furs, had redeemed all of the outstanding wampum with
his labor, and when he went to market to get fire-water, he
was taught that he must have gold and silver to get it.
Then he wanted to ride in blood up to his horses' bridles.
Commerce had found a better tool than wampun had become. The buccaneers and the pirates had brought in
silver, and that defied the Connecticut man's machinery or
the Dutchman's imitations. The years pass by and commerce finds that silver, because of over-production, becomes
uncertain and erratic in value, and with the same instinct
it chooses gold as a standard of value. A coin of unsteady
value is like a knife of uncertain sharpness. It is thrown
aside for one that can do all that is expected of it. Gold is
such a tool. It is the standard of all first-class nations. It
is to-day and it will remain the standard of this republic.

The value of the gold dollar is not in the pictures on it.
It is in the grains of gold in it. Smash it and melt it, and it
buys a hundred cents' worth the world over. Deface a silver dollar and fifty cents of its value goes off yonder among
the silent stars. Free coinage means that the silver miner
may make fifty cents' worth of silver cancel a dollar's worth
of debts. This is a greenback doctrine in a silver capsule.
Bimetallism is a diplomatic term for international use.

Monometallism with silver as the metal is the dream of the Populist and of the poor deluded Democratic grasshoppers who dance by this moonshine until they get frostbitten.

The free silver heresy is about dead. It has cost this country at to-day's price for silver $170,000,000. The few saddened priests of this unhappy fetich who remain active, find their disciples all rallying around the standard of currency reform. The report of the Secretary of the Treasury is a confession of national financial sins, and a profession of faith in sound money doctrines. Every business man will watch with keen interest the progress of the plan for a reform in our currency. You all know that the straight road is the retirement of the greenback and the Treasury note, and the withdrawal of the Government from the banking business, and you will naturally distrust any makeshift measures. The greenback is a war debt, and a debt that is now troublesome. We are funding and refunding it in gold daily, and are still paying it out as currency to come back after gold. Any scheme to sequestrate it, to hide it under a bushel, or to put it under lock and key is a shallow device. The way to retire it is to retire it. It has served its full purpose, and there never was a better time than now to call it in.

In twelve years all of our Government debt matures. The national banking system, based upon it, must expire with it unless existing laws are changed. This system has served the nation well. No one has ever lost a dollar by a national bank note. The system is worth preserving, and with a little more liberal treatment it can be made to serve until a currency, based upon commercial credits and linked to a safety fund, a system which works so admirably in Canada, can be engrafted upon it. There is a great hurry to create such a system now on a basis of the partial sequestration of the greenback and the Treasury note, but the bottom principle is wrong. The Government should discourage a commercial credit currency, based upon a public credit currency, which, in turn, rests upon a slender gold deposit, exposed to every holder of a Government demand note. A credit currency is a double-edged tool, and needs to be handled with great care. We have had so much of crazy-quilt finance that I am sure that we want no more of it. We have been sorely punished for our financial sins in the past, and now that we are repentant, we want to get everything right before we go ahead with our full native energy. We have suffered from the distrust of the world and then from our own distrust. In retracing our steps, let us be sure that we are on solid ground, and make our "wampum" as good as the best.

CHAUNCEY M. DEPEW TO TRAMPS.

On Christmas eve, 1896, Dr. Chauncey M. Depew dined with a New York woman reporter and 50 tramps at the St. Denis hotel, in New York City. Dr. Depew was formally invited, but the tramps were recruited from a long line of nondescript beggars which had formed in front of a bakery across from the St. Denis where bread was being distributed free of charge.

It is Christmas Eve, and I hope we have all begun the hours that lead to Christmas in a proper way—that is, by filling ourselves as full as we can with the good things of this world.

I have presided at many dinners and attended many more—perhaps more than any man in New York—but certainly never did I preside over or attend a dinner from which I have derived more real pleasure than from this dinner here to-night.

The dinners to which I am sometimes invited are for political or patriotic purposes, but usually they have no other object except that the gentlemen who are present, who are, as a rule, workingmen of affairs, desire to be relieved in some way and they take the occasion of a dinner as one that will afford them an opportunity to have a good time.

I have been a student of that method of enjoyment for a great many years. I have read of the great dinners they had in Rome, when a man would spend his entire fortune, great as those fortunes were, to entertain an emperor.

I have also read of the dinners which are told of in the Bible—notably of that great feast given by Belshazzar, which was the most magnificent feast that was ever spread, we are given to understand, but which was brought to a sudden and awful termination by the handwriting on the wall.

But many of the dinners to which I go seem to me to fill no purpose. There are the big feed and the studied orations, and when it is all over the impression it leaves on me is that there are the bores and the bored—the orators being the bores, and the listeners being the bored.

There is only one of the great historical dinners that really interested me. That is the one that is told of in the New Testament, where the guests, failing to answer or sending excuses, the host found his tables unoccupied. Then it was that he told the people of his household to go out in the highways and byways and gather in all whom they might find. I would like to have been at that dinner. I have pictured it often in my mind. Had the guests who had been invited attended, some of them would have criticised the wines of the host, saying they had better in their own cellars; others would have criticised the food and declared that their own cooks could have prepared finer dishes. Then, as he departed, each would shake the hand of the host hypocritically and bid him good-night with the false statement that he never had a better time or a better dinner in his life.

In my mind's eye I can see some of the guests who attended that feast. One was, perhaps, the student who, in striving after distinction in a profession, had neglected to provide for his material wants and was in distress. Another was, perhaps, the skilled mechanic out of a job, wanting only the opportunity to work, but failing to find it. I can picture the lawyer without clients, and the playwright who had grown discouraged because he could not sell his play and had become destitute in his search for a purchaser. I can see there, too, the poet or the author, whom publishers had not recognized, but who was destined to become a great man in the literature of the future. I can see there, too, the professional tramp, who would do everything but work, but absolutely refused to do that. The professional tramp, more completely than any other type of man on earth, meets the biblical description of the lily of the field. He toils not, neither does he spin, yet Solomon, in all his glory was not arrayed like one of these.

We meet here this Christmas eve, and the occasion is one that suggests a few things to me—to all of us. No matter how fortunate or unfortunate we may be, Christmas eve should be an hour of rejoicing. Whether we are in luck or whether we are not in luck, we cannot forget that this hour is the one that led to the coming of Christ to this earth. He came as the great leveler. It was his mission to inculcate doctrines that would wipe out despotism and injustice.

Surely, if we look back at the conditions that prevailed when Christ came on earth and at the conditions to-day, we must admit that the doctrines which he taught mankind have accomplished wonderful results in leveling despotism and injustice. But for those doctrines there never could have been a United States of America. But for those doctrines there never could have been a country where all men were equal in the eyes of the law. But for those doctrines there would never have been institutions of education which the children of all men could enjoy.

If a man has the element of hope in his heart he can and will find a landing place from which he can start afresh in the journey of life, no matter how dark his past has been. You may say that it is easy for a man like me to make such a statement as that.   But, my friends, it has been my privilige during the last thirty years to come in contact with men who have encountered the most discouraging conditions of life.   I have seen men who were in magnificent circumstances go to the gutter through rum.   I have seen them conquer the appetite, and, having conquered it, gain new courage.   I have seen them starting from that new landing place, work up and up again until they reached their proper sphere.

I have a case in mind.   A boy started in life with me up in Peekskill.   In the villages of this State, when I was a boy, all the lads knew each other by their first names and played together.   The brightest fellow among all of the boys became a skilled mechanic, married a beautiful girl, had a lovely home, became foreman of the shop in which he worked, and was in line to become a partner in the concern.   He became imbued with the desire to enter public life.   In his efforts to be a good fellow, and to make those whose favor he sought think that he was, he became a patron of the village saloons.

The taste for liquor was hereditary in that man, and it was not long before he became an outcast, the worst tramp I ever knew, so filthy in himself that he became known throughout the village as "Dirty Blank."   His family left him and his friends forsook him and he drifted to New York.

One night he followed a band of Salvation Army men and women to jeer at them.   In some way they caught him, and it was not long before he was marching with them, beating the drum, and exhorting others to turn from their evil ways as he had done.   As soon as he got on his feet he went back to Peekskill.   His condition was so changed that his wife and children returned to him, his friends lent him a helping hand, and to-day he is justice of the peace there and is highly respected by all who know him.

I know what it is to be in hard luck myself. I belong to a family that has the trait of always worrying about things that don't happen. My father died of worrying, and my grandfather died of worrying, and I had almost made up my mind that I would die of worry. For the first thirty years of my life I worried enough to have shuffled off this mortal coil and climbed the Golden Stairs.

But I had good lungs, good heart, good stomach, and good muscles, and somehow I couldn't die. Then I had a hard blow. I lost every dollar I had in the world. My father was one of those men who believed that a boy should be thrown out into the world to hustle for himself if he was ever going to amount to anything. I went to him with my troubles. All he did was to cry. I did not want tears. I wanted greenbacks. I wanted help, not sympathy.

I thought then that my jig was up for sure, and for a time was very much down in the heart. But I found nothing in that, and one day, thank God, I came to realize that this was a bright and beautiful world. I said to myself that the great majority of people seem to get along in some way, if they did what was right. So I declared that I would go to work, stop worrying, cultivate cheerfulness and try to be merry.

The result of that philosophy is that for twenty years I have been trying to get fun out of everything. If it's work, I get fun out of that. If I am at sea during a hard blow and everybody else is so sick that they wish they were dead, I try to get fun out of that, too. I am always trying to get a chance to laugh. The result is that I have reversed the hereditary conditions which nature put in me, but which God never intended that a man should be afflicted by. I cultivated hope until I became an optimist. I came to believe that to-morrow would be better than to-day, and if to-morrow was not, then I simply believed that it was the wrong day, and that the next day would be better.

I believe that the trouble with most of us is that we get in a rut. We get in the procession, and we cannot get out of it. We want something a little better than the chance that is given to us at the time. We are not willing enough to take the chance that we have presented to us.

Up in Peekskill, a town which originates pretty nearly all the things that are worth thinking about in this world, and in which I had my origin, they used to have a habit in old times of always following a hearse at a funeral. A Peeks-killer who had come down to New York and died, was to be "planted," as Peekskillers say. Some of his New York friends went up to the funeral. They took carriages and got into the procession to follow the hearse. After a while they noticed that they were riding over very rough ground and that the carriage was swaying from side to side in such a manner as to threaten to spill them all out. One of the New York dudes stuck his head out of the carriage window and shouted to the driver:

"Hi, there! What the deuce are you trying to do? Do you want to break our necks? Where are you taking us to, anyway?" The old Peekskill driver leaned over and answered: "Well, I'll tell you, gents, the horses with the hearse started to run away ten minutes ago, and they're running yet, and, you know, up here in Peekskill it's the rule for the mourners to follow the hearse, and I ain't going to break it."

Now, it's not a good rule to follow the hearse. If you've been doing it, stop.

When a man finds himself in the wrong procession, the best thing for him to do is to get out. When the chance comes it may not be at a very inviting landing place, but if it gives him an opportunity, and if he has the courage and pluck, and sobriety to take advantage of it, and does so, he is on the way to make all his Christmases Merry Christmases.

An old friend of mine was to build a line of railroad in the west that is now connected with a system with which I have something to do. He had worked himself up from the bottom and became general manager of a small company. The line which he was engaged to build was through a section of country inhabited by farmers who had never seen a railroad. The line was built, and the train stood on the tracks ready to make the trial trip. A prominent old farmer of the region went to my friend and told him that he had ridden about everything from a bucking broncho to a steer, but he had never ridden a railroad, and he'd like to do it. So he was invited on that trial trip. The train whizzed along and he was mighty amazed. He happened to look out of the window just as the train was crossing a trestle. Seeing no ground underneath him, he became badly frightened and fell on his knees in an attitude of prayer. My friend looked at him for a minute and said:

"Why, Farmer Smith, what's the matter with you? What are you doing?"

"Well," said the old farmer, "I'm praying to the Lord that when this old train lights and smashes I will be spared."

So it is with many of us as we travel on the train of life. We look out and we see no ground under us and we fear a smash. But we are really on a trestle, and if we'll push along we'll get on solid ground again.

I wish you one and all a Merry Christmas to-morrow, and an opportunity to work and to prosper during the coming year. I wish from the bottom of my heart that you will all start out to-night with new hope.

My own experience has taught me that when one has nothing but good luck in life he does not amount to much. In every knockdown there is a lesson which teaches us to avoid rocks over which we have fallen. The road is full of these rocks, but after a time we learn to avoid them, and every time that a man arises after a serious fall and realizes that he is still strong enough to push on the element of hope becomes a stronger part of his nature.

"THE FEDERAL JUDICIARY."

Response of Judge P. S. Grosscup, of Chicago, at a banquet of the Illinois Bar, July 16, 1896.

I had intended to grow eloquent on this subject until I heard the last speaker, and he has taught me that common sense is the acme of judicial virtue. After hearing General Black this morning on "John Marshall," I must confess I would rather have his career than any other. He has influenced development in this country far more than either Washington or Lincoln. They were part of the great movements of their time. John Marshall was a great movement in himself, and built the judicial structure of which we are the heirs and beneficiaries. When the constitutional convention was held in 1777, only the seed was planted, and no one knew to what a growth it would come. In Marshall's mind alone was the seed germinated which has brought forth what we call America.

Marshall was the personification of the federal judiciary. It was Marshall and the Supreme Court of the United States that developed all those great qualities which mark the republic's achievements. The clause that the law of the United States should be the supreme law of the land was Marshall's. Out of that has grown the great system by which the Supreme Court of the United States lays hands on all others, consolidates and unifies all judicial tribunals of this country, preventing any locality from tarnishing or destroying the national honor; that has developed all the transportation facilities of this land so that they have been made a single department of a central government. I see among us our senior Senator, and I say to him and to you that, in my judgment, the man who has given this clause the first legislative sanction has a place more resplendent than eight years of the presidency will give him.

We have fallen on times which may seem somewhat strange. The judiciary of the United States had to bear, however, much from popular clamor and fanaticism 100 years ago. It is to Marshall and the Supreme Court of the United States that I owe it that my allegiance has not to travel through Springfield before it reaches Washington. If I violate the law of the country, the punishment comes from Washington direct.

The judiciary of the United States represents the great middle class—the bulk of the population between the criminal rich and the restless poor, who, after all, are the salt and savor of our institutions. No man in America has the monopoly of humanitarianism. The federal judiciary cannot mark equality, but it can make conditions better. We are continually going upward. From bivouac to bivouac we climb still to a greater height in our march of progress. Humanity is not going to Calvary. It is on the road to the culmination of the teachings of Him who on the hills of Galilee said: "Go forth and teach all the world what I have told you." Humanity is not going forth to be crucified on a cross of gold nor to wear a crown of thorns. It is going upward toward that golden effulgence of humanity's resurrection morning.

"THE ADVOCATE."

Response by J. J. McCarthy, of Duluth, at the Iowa State Bar Association Banquet, at Des Moines, Iowa, July 20, 1896.

In a broad and popular sense the advocate is a person authorized and permitted by law to argue cases in court. In Great Britain the distinction is clearly made between the counselor and the advocate—the counselor never trying a cause to court or jury, this being the province of the advocate. But in this country the distinction is abolished. Here the advocate is the lawyer and the lawyer is the advocate. The terms are synonymous. The duties of the one are inseparable from those of the other. The relations of each are the same. In the few minutes that are allotted, instead of attempting to discuss the art of presenting causes in court and jury, the methods of proper and successful procedure in trials of actions, I prefer to make a few general observations, which in the presence of recent occurrences, as appears to me are suitable to the subject assigned.

A study of the advocate of the past—the advocate, the lawyer, of the old school—the contemporary of Blackstone and of Chitty, or Webster and of Choate, challenges our admiration and should demand our greatest respect. In these modern times of resolutions and platforms, of whereases and harangues, of insinuations and epithets, coming from large assemblages of our people, where the advocate, the lawyer, nay, even the judges of the highest court on earth, are referred to with distrust and disfavor; when to be a lawyer, and especially a corporation lawyer, is, in the opinion of many, a sufficient disqualification for political preferment, we of the profession should not sit idly by without inquiring the cause. This seems to be a modern tendency, and in the light of passing events cannot and should not be overlooked by the bench and bar of the time.

In times past the advocate, the lawyer, instead of being held up as a person to be shunned, distrusted and avoided, was the special recipient of political, business and social preferment. And why not? In those times none were permitted to appear in court in behalf of a client to plead the cause of right and truth, but men of the highest character and integrity, men of pure, patriotic and honest lives, possessed of lofty and noble traits, educated, learned men, who held culture, refinement and patriotism and personal honor above mere success and worldly gain; above everything. In those times advocacy was a profession, not a trade; it was a science, not a commercial enterprise. The advocate was at once counselor, guardian, teacher, friend. He must, above all and beyond all, be a man of the most perfect integrity; this was the first and most essential requirement. He was obliged, without pay, to give the utmost care and attention to every detail of his client's cause; he must correctly and honestly, before appearing in court, explain to his client the law and at his peril warn him of the least transgression of it; he must never undertake a cause which may seem to himself unjust or dishonest, nor at any cost must he permit himself to be made the instrument of spite, malice or ill will. Unpleasant truths, when necessary of expression, were couched in language of commendable forbearance and modesty which always bespoke the true gentleman. The betraying of a professional secret or the making use of professional information for pecuniary gain or other ignoble purposes, though seldom occurrences, were cursed and despised. A violation in the slightest degree of any of these rules and requirements was always punshed, which in every instance amounted to removal from practice before the courts, and often by fine and imprisonment, besides. In those days the breach of a professional trust, the advocacy of a known dishonest and unjust cause or the gaining of a case by unscrupulous means were not only loathed and hated by the public, but the judges upon the bench and the legal profession saw to it that there was visited upon the wrongdoer the full penalties of the law. In those days the violation of a law of the land had some meaning; and the violation of the law of the land by the advocate or lawyer met with as sure and certain a punishment as did that of the humblest citizen; and the infraction of a rule of professional ethics was invariably followed by professional dishonor and condemnation from bench and bar.

After continuing his eloquent tribute to the practitioner of former days at some length, Mr. McCarthy proceeded:

History bears evidence of the truth of all I have said of the advocate of the last century. And notwithstanding mutterings of discontent and the severe public and private criticisms that are heard concerning the lawyer of to-day, yet it is safe to assert that the great majority of the American lawyers now at the bar, although surrounded by different and more tempting environments, are as honest, able, honorable and patriotic as those that have gone before them in any age or time. It is the dishonest and disreputable pettifogging trickster that brings disgrace and distrust upon the profession. The one who packs a jury and suborns witnesses but wins his case, makes money, holds his positions of honor and moves in good society, is the person who robs the true advocate of his rightful place and brings unmerited condemnation upon the profession. The advocate whose purpose is to win his cause by fair or foul means, takes or gives a bribe, and yet continues at the bar and fraternizes with his fellows in the profession, is the man who is known and talked about in the community. In short, the unreliable trickster is known to everyone and, unlike his fellows in former times, is tolerated at the bar without scarcely a word of protest or reproach from the reputable members of the profession. He should be disbarred and removed from practice and exposed to the public gaze. The public, however, is much to blame. How often in this age of commercial enterprise, in this time of worship of the almighty dollar, do we hear the standing and the ability of the advocate measured by the cases he has won in court —the number of verdicts he has secured. No question is made as to the means employed to win this case. He won it, and that's all that's to it. It may be a trick, it may be by intentional concealment of facts, it may be by some imposition upon the judge, it may be by packing the jury or the manufacturing of perjured testimony or an appeal to the baser passions of men. Such verdicts are barren victories. They bring merited disgrace upon lawyers, courts and juries. The lawyer that will resort to such methods does not deserve the name of lawyer. He should be disbarred as well as punished, and the time-honored profession to which we belong owe it to themselves and to the public to take a step forward in this direction.

In other countries the judges upon the bench are looked to by the reputable members of the profession for protection against the corrupt and dishonest. But there they have an independent judiciary, free from the influences of the ward caucus and the political lawyer. The judges upon our benches, although generally men of high character and ability, are only members of the bar selected for a time from among their fellows, and too often they find it to their interest to pass over without notice gross violations of law and legal ethics. Such, in my opinion, are the things that bring ridicule, denunciation and distrust upon the profession at large. But the public should remember that such conduct is the exception, not the rule. The profession should not be condemned because of the transgressions of a few of its members. The true advocate is he that with honest and high-minded motives appeals to the court or jury for a just and fair disposition of his client's cause; he that in every way possible endeavors to enlighten the court or jury on the law and facts in the case; he who looks upon the judge as the sworn and impartial administrator of justice, rather than a partisan referee in a game of chance; he that accords to the jury their historic and time-honored province as guardians of the liberties of the common people as against the avarice of man and the tyranny of rulers; he that looks upon jurors as men of integrity and common sense, rather than as men selected to decide questions of fact according to their prejudices or as personal favors to friends; he that conceives his true province to be the obtaining from courts and juries of just and honest decisions; he that maintains in the spirit and letter of our own statute the respect due to the courts of justice, that advocates or counsels no actions or defenses except those which appear to him legal and just, who employs only such means as are consistent with truth, who never under any possible circumstances seeks to mislead the judge upon the bench by any artifice, false statement of fact or law, or by any indirection or trick, who holds sacred the confidence and secret of his client, who abstains from offensive personalities, who in the trial of a cause advances no fact or argument to the prejudice of honor or reputation of a witness or a party, who never encourages the pressing of a cause before a court from any motive of interest or passion, and who never rejects, for considerations personal to himself, the cause of the poor, defenseless or oppressed.

"NEBRASKA HARVEST."

"The vintage is ripe, the harvest is heaping,
But some that have sowed have no riches for reaping."
—Thomas Hood.

Response by E. M. Bartlett, of Omaha, at a complimentary dinner to the millers of Nebraska, given by the Bemis Omaha Bag Company, at Omaha, Neb., August 31, 1896.

Mr. Toastmaster and Fellow Millers:

While I am deeply sensible of the honor of being invited to this magnificent spread, I was at a loss to know why I should be asked to speak at a dinner where practical millers are supposed to carry off the honors. I explained to Mr. Peters, your genial host, when invited to speak, that I was not a miller but a lawyer. He informed me that I was the same as a mill. I asked him how he made that out, and he replied to me: "You are a high roller and will grind all right with the lubricating you will receive at the banquet." At this suggestion I surrendered. When I look over the list of gentlemen here, who were selected to address this company, I congratulate myself that I am not the only one whose grinding process consists solely in that which nature has supplied, and I can understand the fine discriminating care with which he has fitted and adjusted the several parts of the machinery of this mill, so, you see, the mill is justified in thus addressing the miller.

"Nebraska's Harvest." In view of Nebraska's bountiful crop of 1896 I feel that I have been assigned to an exceedingly fertile field. I wish I could do it justice.

In the farmer's life the harvest is that period of solemn work from which the profits or losses, the reward or penalty, attached to toil and labor are ascertained. It is that time which demonstrates whether the husbandman, so to speak, shall gather "grapes of thorns or figs of thistles." "What shall the harvest be?" is the ever anxious inquiry from seed time down to storing the product in the granaries. The devout old lady expressed the idea, when driving past one of those beautifully and regularly planted cornfields, the seemingly convergent, pennoned rows standing in graceful, waving uniformity, appearing to the eye as all such cornfields do, beautiful beyond description when sown with a lister, she remarked, "The corn groweth where 'tis listed, but whether there will be a crop or not the Lord only knows."

Formerly the farmer's capacity for grain raising was limited to the necessities of his family for food and seeding purposes. The miler ground his grain into flour for home consumption merely. Then no one could rob the farmer but the cheerful, plump and lusty miller—and he wouldn't. This is why the miller is erroneously handed down to us in poetry and song as both honest and jolly, two qualities which, according to Shakespere, do not always fraternize in the same individual, but which, nevertheless, we must admit are concordant in the breast of each guest here tonight.

Modern invention has developed the farmer's capacity for cultivating the field, so that now he feeds the world.

He no longer takes the result of the harvest to the miller
in a large bag on horseback, grain on one side and stone
ballast on the other, but to the advance agent of the miller,
the grain buyer, and he in turn to that mysterious structure
by the railroad track that elevates the product but not the
price, and to the individual the product of the harvest there-
after becomes a myth—a sort of iridescent, scintillating will
o' the wisp, or like the wind, "It bloweth where it listeth, and
thou hearest the sound thereof, but canst not tell whence it
cometh and whither it goeth." It changes ownership without delivery. Men buy it without seeing the object of their
purchase, unload it without the aid of brawn or shovel, and
have nothing to prove the deal save the burden of loss; but
eventually it finds its way, as if by magic, to the mill, and
I fear that under the new roller process the farmer, the
buyer, the miler, and all, except the mammoth mills, are
ground in the milling. And finally it appears transfigured
upon our tables, the staff of life, and it glides into our deeper
self with a mild and gentle sympathy that steals away the
sharpness of its journey thither ere we are aware.

"The Harvest." The poet and historian have surrounded the hardships incident to sowing the seed and
"gathering in the sheaves" with all the consolation that
magnificent word painting can produce, but the husbandman in the operation of his farm has, in a practical way, surpassed the poet in his most lofty flights of imagination. He
rides his plow, his harrow, his seeder, his harvester, with all
the grace, dignity and complaisance of the muses on their
winged Pegasus. No more does the ancient barn floor,
strewn with shining straw, respond to the music of the flail.
The cradle and the flail are things of the past, and even the
old threshing machine, once so cumbersome and rebellious,
wooed now by the magic and seductive fascinations of steam
and electricity, surrenders all and does the work of horse
and man. Now the harvest is looked forward to not as

that time when, after it is garnered, the husbandman may sink into hopeful contemplation, in the gentle stillness of October days, and see visions of plenty surrounded by mirth and happiness, but as the time when the sale of the product shall enrich the laborer, make him worthy of his hire and powerful among his fellows.

May the farmer have riches for his reaping, and let us hope by some good stroke of fortune large crops may be accompanied by liberal prices to the husbandman and to the miller. I wish that every grain of "Nebraska's Harvest" could be ground in Nebraska roller mills.

The toast suggests another harvest which has been gathered in this State the harvest of glory and honor that has been bestowed by the nation upon young Nebraska's favored sons. This is a non-political and non-sectarian company. We may therefore feel a just pride in this harvest without respect to party or creed. A. U. Wyman, of Omaha, was Treasurer of the United States during two separate periods, under Presidents Grant, Hayes, Garfield, Arthur and Cleveland. Our townsman, Chares F. Manderson, who graced the position of United States Senator from Nebraska for twelve years, was chosen as its President by the United States Senate. J. Sterling Morton, of Nebraska City, one of our honored guests this evening, is now a member of the President's Cabinet as Secretary of Agriculture of the United States. In this year of our Lord Charles E. Bentley, of Lincoln, was chosen by the National Prohibition Convention which met at Pittsburg, Penn., in May. John M. Thurston, of Omaha, present junior United States Senator, was chosen chairman of the National Republican Convention, which met at St. Louis in June. William J. Bryan, of Lincoln, ex-Congressman from Nebraska, was nominated by the Democratic-Populist National Convention at Chicago, in July, for President of the United States. William V. Allen, of Madison, our senior United States

Senator from Nebraska, was made chairman of the National Populist Convention at St. Louis, in July. The presidency of the Commercial Law League of America was bestowed upon an Omaha citizen at the National Convention which met at Omaha in July. James M. Woolworth, of Omaha, was elected President of the American Bar Association which met at Saratoga in August, and it is said that our townsman, Thaddeus S. Clarkson, will be elected Commander-in-Chief of the Grand Army of the Republic at Minneapolis this month. Even the Pope of Rome has sought Nebraska and given the highest honor ever conferred by the Church upon an American citizen—the title of Count, granted to our honored citizen and townsman, John A. Creighton.

We may feel that, with such a harvest of distinguished honors, our young Commonwealth is one of the brightest stars in the galaxy of States,—Nebraska, whose fertile soil yields more wealth in grain than is produced by the mineral output from other States; "whose sons are all boys and whose daughters are all girls;" the fame of whose statesmen and financiers is coëxtensive with the boundaries of the globe, and whose orators have demonstrated, and are still demonstrating, that even the zephyrs from Heaven have no monopoly on wind. I have endeavored to follow the time-honored custom of occasions like this, of talking as far from the subject as possible, and now, in conclusion, I desire to propose this sentiment for our guests: "The millers of Nebraska: May they never grind the poor nor be ground themselves. May all the ends they aim at be the hopper, the best flour and largest profits."

"BROTHERHOOD OF RAILROAD BRAKEMEN."

Response by W. W. Dodge, at Burlington, Iowa, at a banquet given at the National Convention of the Brotherhood of Railroad Brakemen, in the City of Burlington, Iowa, October 19, 1885.

Mr. President, Delegates, Ladies and Gentlemen :

I deem this a most interesting occasion and an honor to be invited to address you. The assembling of delegates of the "Brotherhood of Railroad Brakemen" in our beautiful city, at their annual reunion, is a compliment to this metropolis. The freedom of our city and the hand of welcome have been extended in a fitting manner by our chief executive. The history of this association, its phenomenal growth, its splendid membership, the good that it has done, its promising future, have been descanted upon in words like "apples of gold set in pictures of silver" by the eloquent gentlemen who have preceded me. I am, therefore, something like a mariner at sea without a compass, at a loss to know what course to pursue. As a last hope I turn to your motto, "Benevolence, Sobriety, Industry," as the chart from which I will take my bearings.

Industry, though last named, is one of the brightest beacon lights of your trinity of principles, is a foundation rock of your order. It must run like a silver thread through all your actions if you would reach the grand results aimed at by your brotherhood. It is the water-wheel that runs your institution; lower the supply the wheel becomes silent, the mill idle. I can safely assert that nine-tenths of the brakemen of this country are young men. Therefore, a fellow feeling prompts me to address my remarks particularly to you.

The all-wise Being has seen proper to create no two persons exactly alike; no two leaves in the forest similar in all their parts; no two things in nature one the precise counterpart of the other. As our physical forms are different, so are our mental attributes, personal character, ambitions, inclinations and desires of the heart. It is in the morning of youth that the future man is molded. Thus it is essential during youth's development and when the mind is best capable of being guided for good or evil, that you shape your destiny and select your part in the great drama of life. If you are not imbued with the true spirit of industry and morality, inspired with lofty aspirations and ambitions, you may well write your prospects of success upon the running waters. It is said, "Cultivate the physical exclusively and you have an athlete or a savage, the moral only, you have an enthusiast or a maniac; the intellectual only, you have a diseased oddity, it may be a monster. It is only by wisely training all three together that the complete man can be formed." Forget not this rule. "Take care of the moments and the hours will take care of themselves."

Your occupation is a peculiar one; while on duty your moments are busily employed, but when off you have long hours of rest. It is during this period of bodily and mental quiet recreation that your passions, like the smoldering volcano, are liable to burst forth and master your better judgment. Thus it may be while under the shadow of the demon's wing you may violate the second cardinal principle of your brotherhood. Remember, "This above all; to thine own self be true, and it must follow as the night the day, thou can'st not then be false to any man."

Laws are made to protect our rights and redress our wrongs. The State is willing to shield us in the enjoyment of "life, liberty and the pursuit of happiness," yet it makes no provision to protect the widow and orphan. What a consoling thought it must be to a member of your order to know that should dread disease, or unexpected accident call you to the land beyond, the strong right arm of your brotherhood will be thrown around your loved ones and bring them aid, solace and comfort. Be true to your order, for it is the cross to which your wife and child must cling when the dreadful hour of final separation arrives, the ark in which they take refuge when alone on the tempestuous waves of life's uncertain sea.

The daily routine work of a brakeman is filled with hazard and danger. Yet, willingly, fearlessly, he performs it. He knows that "when duty calls it is his to obey." Observe him at his post, ever on the alert. When earth is immersed in Egyptian darkness or when in noonday sunlight he acts, he labors amid the perils of his chosen vocation. What is that sound? It is the shriek of the whistle, he grasps his lantern, out through the window he springs, runs over the sleet-covered cars, faces the fierce, merciless winds, turns the brakes, returns to his post ready to respond to the next call of duty, be it the particular switch to turn, or the dangerous coupling to make. So his work goes on until the watchful eye of a superior, appreciating moral, industrious habits, advances him a round on the ladder of promotion. That a young railroad man, combining perseverance and industry, can reach the topmost round is amply illustrated in the life and success of the manager of the greatest line of railroad that runs through our State.

History is also replete with instances where from humble parentage and the lowly walks of life young men have risen to the highest pinnacle of fame. There is Captain Cook, the circumnavigator of the globe, born in a mud hut, and started in life as a cabin boy. Admiral Nelson was a coxswain in his youth. Lord Eldon, the son of a coal merchant. Franklin, the philosopher, was the son of a half-starved weaver. Heyne, the renowned German scholiast, was born in a poor peasant's cot. Burns, the bard of Scotland, ate the coarse bread of labor. The youthful poet, Kirke White, was the son of a butcher. Whitefield, the renowned pulpit orator, was the son of a tavern keeper. Lincoln was a rail-splitter; Grant, a tanner; Cleveland, the humble preacher's son, and many other most encouraging illustrations.

"Brotherhood of Railroad Brakemen," you have my sincerest wish for your future prosperity. I live in the hope to see your order take its place among the great benevolent societies of this country, second to none. Your benevolent, charitable deeds shine forth in this working-day life as the stars in heaven. Let the glory of God run like a golden thread through all your actions and you will stand forth before the world, loved and respected by your fellow men.

"ST. VALENTINE."

Response by W. W. Dodge, of Burlington, Iowa, at a reception and banquet given by the Des Moines Press Club, at Hotel Aborn, Des Moines, Iowa, February 14, 1888.

The perspective of the past is pictured with many beautiful legends and traditions. The antiquities of the common people form an interesting study. It is said by the eminent writer, John Brand, "that by the chemical process of philosophy, even wisdom may be extracted from the follies and superstitions of our forefathers." The dim light from the candles of long ago often causes the student to despair in seeking the origin of the superstitious notions and ceremonies of the people. Though the fountain head of the streams which have carried these traditions down the centuries may never be reached, still there is enough on the charts of other lands to indicate where they were first perceived to flow.

In responding to the toast, "St. Valentine," I may be permitted to recall the tradition of "Valentine's Day." It is said that there is unquestionable authority to show that the custom of choosing valentines was a sport practiced in the houses of the gentry of England as early as in the year 1476. In England, Scotland, and Lorraine and Maine in France, the eve of the 14th of February was celebrated by a very peculiar and amusing custom. An equal number of maids and bachelors would assemble together, and write the names of acquaintances upon little billets, which they deposited in a vessel. The maids would then draw the men's billets and the men the maids'. The person thus drawn becomes one's valentine. Fortune thus having divided the company into so many couples, the valentines give balls and engage in other festivities. Upon these occasions they wear their billets upon their bosoms or sleeves, and this little sport often ended in love and a happy marriage.

St. Valentine's Day still remains with us as one of the most popular of festivals. The young, of to-day, and may I not include the silver locks, feel still a throbbing of the heart on the eve of that to-morrow which may bring them a valentine. The care and sorrow, and the weary toil of a busy life, is brushed aside by memories of this day. The father, the mother, receives a valentine from their ringlet-crowned boy. It is a dear, little billet of love, from the sweetest creature, to them, on earth. He sends another to a blue-eyed playmate. He had thought of her, for he wrote with childish trembling her name on this white-winged messenger. For the time, thoughts of hobby-horses, marbles and ball are displaced by the outlines of a fancy, a vision, a dream just forming, and here can it not be said that the light of a pure, holy love is just entering the soul. A few years are hidden by the hills, and the "lips of the boy in a love kiss unite with the lips of the maid whom his bosom holds dear." Pardon me, I must draw the curtain, for you all know how it ends.

For some days past the windows of the storekeeper have had, almost, the appearance of a fairy grotto—valentines, beautiful in design, dazzling with gilt and silver, have attracted the attention of the passer-by. The society belle dressed so richly and warmly in ermine, the humble factory girl in calico and light shawl, obviously stand shoulder to shoulder, reading the mottoes and verses on these ready messengers.

It is an assumption of mine, though based on no tradition, and I doubt whether it can be found in the books, that the modern "society paper" can serve the purpose of a valentine. Have you ever had the pleasure to glance at its tinted pages, and then soberly reflect upon the verses, and the sweet culled flowers from the realm of prose, therein contained? Have you not anxiously scanned its columns to see whether your toilet had been properly described, and your personal appearance duly appreciated by a competent judge? for, as Byron poetically has it:

> "'Tis pleasant, sure, to see one's name in print;
> A book's a book, altho' there's nothing in't."

You will not be doing violence to your "distracted globe" by harboring the thought that from such as these the world may gain another Meredith, Ik Marvel or Lord Byron. Again, I must beg your kindly indulgence, and merciful criticism, while I continue to harmonize and endeavor to apply the thought of the valentine to the modern newspaper, and its editor.

I first must request you to visit with me a sanctum in which an embryo Horace Greeley is busily at work. With great hazard to life and limb, in ascending to the top story, a winding passage, for all the world like the catacombs of Rome, we finally reach his august presence. He is there. Also the scissors and paste pot; but, oh, what an odor. Does it resemble the ravishing perfume of "Pyrrhus," "May Flowers," "New Mown Hay," or the indescribable odor from the famous vessels of China? Recovering from our semi-asphyxiated condition, we take the liberty to gaze upon his expansive brow, reaching from his chin to the collar button on the back of his neck. His unwashed hand rests upon this broad, comprehensive dome, "as motionless as a painted ship on a painted ocean." He is thinking. He is endeavoring to lasso his thoughts which have stampeded, like a herd of Texas steers. Well, he grabs a pencil and endeavors to head off the "Leader" by "Register"-ing a "News" item, which is a "Capital" idea. The fleeing thoughts are corralled, and with the rapidity of a trip-hammer he pounds the white paper and blackens it all over with carbon marks. We have become interested, as page after page of "copy" is thrown behind, like miles after a "G-whiz train." Fearing that perpetual motion may set in, we timidly approach, and for the sake of information ask him the pertinent question, in kind of a moralizing way, "What, sir, eventually becomes of the thoroughly wicked and depraved?" He looked up, thought a moment, and said, "They will edit a country newspaper for a little while, and eventually go to the Legislature." I hazarded another question. It was this: "I presume you find editing a newspaper a very lucrative employment, and as a consequence you must necessarily live in a brown-stone front, surrounded by all the comforts of life?" He slowly shook his head, and without saying a word, reached for his hip pocket—"it" wasn't there, he had left it at home on the piano wrapped up in a lace handkerchief. Concluding that the tongue is mightier than the pistol, he avenged himself by telling us a story. "Listen," he gently murmured. "Once upon a time a bold, bad burglar, of the 'Jim the Climber' sort, appreciating that the editor of a newspaper is the chief man in a town, presumed him also to be very rich. He entered the editor's house one night, and after searching in vain for gold watches, currency and diamond rings without success, it flashed upon him that he had wronged the supposed millionaire, so, opening his heart, he thereupon generously slipped $1.25 into the pocket of the sleeping editor. Next morning when the editor discovered the great wealth that had been thust upon him, he almost fainted with ecstatic joy. He at once thought that it had been quietly placed in his pocket by a good and rich neighbor, who owned a big distillery and lectured on temperance. So, for weeks, he filled his columns with choicest editorials in praise of this good man, who was elected to the Legislature, and ever after the two men were the best of friends. Thus do good actions always meet their reward."

Come, now, let us leave his presence, for soon the sun will begin to "brush away the stars," and the merry voices of the newsboys will be heard to cry out, "Here's your morning paper." "All about John L. Sullivan's flirtation with the Queen of England," "James G. Blaine telegraphs that he is not a candidate for President, but he will get there just the same," "President Cleveland has defined the main issue for the next national election," "All about Senator Finn's great speech favoring the railroads of Iowa." And thus the news from all countries enters our home each morning with as much relish and fond pleasure as bachelors and maids receive their valentines on this day. In our wild, mad rush down the hill of life, we seldom stop to think of the labor, expense and thankless efforts of the press in the up-building of our communities. Some regard them as "common carriers," and that it is the duty of the paper to do this, and say that, all for the "dear people's sake," and may it not be truthfully said that the people, like republics, are sometimes ungrateful. Here we see a candidate for office, lifted by the press from the utmost depths of obscurity to the topmost round of the ladder of fame, where ofttimes stands Fortune with her horn of plenty. From his lofty perch he forgets to look down the valley to those little "printing offices" where men of genius and brains first blazed the trail and then made clear his way.

I conclude with the beautiful and eloquent words borrowed from Thackeray in speaking of the "press:"

"There she is; she never sleeps. She has her ambassadors in every quarter of the world—her couriers upon every road. Her officers march along with the armies, and her envoys into statesmen's cabinets. They are ubiquitous,

Yonder journal has an agent at this moment giving bribes at Madrid, and another inspecting the price of potatoes at Covent Garden."

"THE SACRED MISTLETOE."

Response by W W. Dodge, at a banquet given on the occasion of the Thirty-seventh Annual State Convention of the United Ancient Order of Druids of Iowa, at Burlington, Iowa, June 14, 1893.

Members of the Ancient Order of Druids, Ladies and Gentlemen:

The military law teaches us that the first duty of the soldier is to obey. It is, therefore, in briefly addressing you, like a true soldier, I perform the pleasing duty assigned me by the local committee of Druids.

In 1856, ten years after Iowa had cast aside her territorial dress for that of Statehood, the Druidical pioneers planted the first Grove of Druids in the fertile bosom of this Commonwealth, here in the city of Burlington. This city was then the gateway through which civilization passed to the wonderful country situated in this great northwest. Is it then a matter of wonderment that in Burlington, thirty-seven years ago, the first Grove of the United Ancient Order of Druids should have been established? As our fathers in those days welcomed the brotherhood of Druids and helped plant the first Grove in Iowa, we, the sons of those grand old pioneers, propose to extend to you, one and all, the same sincere, hearty and cordial greeting as those of our parents in the days of '56·

I am not honored with a membership in your Order, and therefore cannot speak to you as a brother. Though I have never been led through the labyrinths of a Druids' Grove, and have never sat beneath the sacred oak entwined with the mystic mistletoe and participated in a sacrifice, yet it is my pleasure, as a non-member, to join in these festivities. The pleasures and enjoyments of this day serve in part to commemmorate those of your Druid fathers of long ago, who, at certain seasons of the year, with formal and pompous ceremony, as soon as the sacred mistletoe was discovered entwining the no less sacred oak, collected in large numbers about the tree; a banquet and sacrifice was prepared; a priest in white vestments cut the twig with a golden sickle; two other white-robed priests caught it in a white cloak; two milk-white heifers were instantly offered up, and the remainder of the day was spent in rejoicing.

Astonishment meets us when we undertake the task of tracing the history and origin of the Order of Druids. Especially is this so as they did not allow their tenets and history to be committed to writing. Yet history traces this sect of people to the year 42 B. C. They founded the city of Lyons in the days of the Roman empire, a city which for a time was the most flourishing in Gaul. Through their influence civilization made rapid progress in the provinces, and their schools became famous, and rivalled those of Greece and Italy. In the history of Julius Caesar we find that the whole political power of Gaul was divided between the Druids and the Knights and Nobles. The Druids were not only ministers and teachers of religion, but were judges of the law, and physicians of the people. They were esteemed for their culture and intelligence, and their influence over the people was almost supreme. It is said of them that they were the first to teach of the immortality of the soul and adoration of one Supreme Being. They also believed in the future state of rewards and punishments. They professed "to reform morals, to secure peace, and to encourage goodness," yet they were superstitious, and made use of their magical knowledge. A branch, or one of the triads of the Druids, was known as the Bards. They were supposed to be divinely inspired, and their influence everywhere was very great. They were exempted from military obligations, and passed their lives in the solitude of the forests, engaged in theological and metaphysical studies and meditations.

The Druids finally lost their power and influence during the reign of Emperor Claudius, and were finally driven from their country, and fled to the mountains of Scotland and Wales.

And thus it is the modern Druids meet in Groves, and their lodge rooms are supposed to represent a Grove, the Chief Druid being seated under the sacred oak having the sacred mistletoe entwined in its branches.

The Druids of to-day have embodied in their ritual the teachings and tenets of this once powerful and honored sect. It is a claim, well founded in history, that their work is more ancient than that of any secret organization now in existence, their teachings more beautiful and their songs more inspiring than was ever wafted through the Cedars of Lebanon.

In 1781 the Druids assumed their present character in England. The Order was introduced in the United States in 1830 by the organization of George Washington Grove No. 1, in New York city. From this parent tree groves have sprung up in about every State and Territory in this Union, besides the principal countries in Europe and Australia.

The foundation stones of Druidism are reasoning and sound morality. Social distinctions are ignored and anyone can become a member who loves virtue and abhors vice. It seems to unite men together for mutual protection and improvement. It fosters a spirit of fraternity and good fellowship, makes provision for the care of its sick and the families of its dead members, striving to place them beyond the need of charity.

I trust that much good will come from this, your Thirty-seventh Annual Assemblage, that from this day on your membership will largely increase, that your fraternal ties will be strengthened, that your considerate and brotherly care for the widow and children of a deceased brother will never wane, that each and every one of you and your brothers that are to be will always find shelter and protection amidst your Groves of Sacred Oaks, entwined with the mistletoe, whose very tendril will have inscribed your watchwords, "Unity, Peace and Concord."

"THE LADIES."

Response by W. W. Dodge, at a Bar Banquet at Burlington, Ia., Dec. 30, 1886.

Not yet having been initiated in the Brotherhood of Benedicts, a greater latitude may be allowed me in commenting on this sweet sentiment. You are well aware that at our secret meeting there took place an animated discussion as to whether or not the ladies should be invited to be present at this banquet. A majority verdict decided that the fair ones must stay at home. As I was heartily in favor of having the winsome daughters of Eve with us at this festal board, I do not hold myself responsible to you married men for the private reception tendered you by your faithful, loving wives upon your arrival home. Whether that meeting was one fragrant with essence of love, fresh plucked kisses and caresses a la mode, or a veritable tempest in a teapot. I must ask of each of you to enter your own plea, whether it be one of confession and avoidance or autre fois acquit. Whatever may have been the punishment affixed for this, to me, unpardonable offense, I take it that your better half has tempered justice with mercy and suspended sentence for this night, as all you recalcitrants appear to be here.

We who are in the unhappy state of single misery, by the act of you married men are denied the double compound, triple extract, indescribable, ecstatic joy of having Burlington's fair daughters by our sides, that they might take part in this feast of reason and flow of soul. Aye!

that they might, like bees, "hang upon the eloquence of thy tongue," be dazzled by the scintillations of thy wit, and the roses on their cheeks dewed with thy pathetic utterances.

The verdict of the majority in this case is a cruel one. Further deponent saith not. You lords of creation demur to the ladies' recreations, complain about their "coffees," "lunches," "afternoon teas," "kettle drums," would deny them the pleasure of a little gossip, to talk about Professor Foster's predictions, the fashions, and the dear boys downtown. You would have them stay at home, as "idle as a painted ship upon a painted ocean."

"The ladies—though lost to sight, to memory dear." Sublime sentiment—would that I might pluck sweet flowers of thought from the garden of Meredith and with them fittingly portray it!

The volumes of history are filled with her deeds of daring on the tented fields, and missions of charity and love, in the great hospitals. The galleries of art and science are adorned with her rare productions; the caskets of literature gemmed with pearls of her genius.

The subject to which I am responding is so sweet and interesting that I would like to continue longer, but the toastmaster has given the signal for me to stop, and, therefore, in brief conclusion, may I say, though the ladies be lost to sight, I am sure that, owing to this banquet, to some of you their memory will be dear.

"HANCOCK, THE SUPERB."

Response by W. W. Dodge, at a G. A. R. Campfire, Burlington, Iowa, December 18, 1887.

Members of the G. A. R., Ladies and Gentlemen:

An invitation was extended to me yesterday by a committee of the G. A. R. to deliver, at this "Campfire," a five-minute address, the subject given me: "Hancock, the Superb." I bow at the mention of that renowned name. I deem it the highest privilege to be permitted to express my admiration for this great military genius; one whose name and character are gilded with a lustrous glory of everlasting fame.

Winfield Scott Hancock was born near Norristown, Montgomery County, Pennsylvania, on the 14th of February, 1824. At the age of sixteen he was appointed a cadet at West Point, graduated in June, 1844, and was immediately commissioned brevet second lieutenant in the Sixth Infantry. He served two years with his regiment in the Indian Territory. He distinguished himself in the Mexican war, and the Florida Indian war. On the 21st of September, 1861, he was commissioned Brigadier-General of Volunteers. His military career in the late war of the rebellion is familiar to all. His brilliant campaigns, personal daring, and great victories sound more like stories of knightly emprise than the sober chronicles of modern warfare. Does not the heart of the American youth thrill with justifiable pride at the recital of Hancock's glorious victories, triumphant marches, wonderful achievements upon the battlefields of Antietam, Fredericksburg, Chancellorsville, Williamsburg, Spottsylvania, Gettysburg, Cold Harbor, and many other sanguinary engagements. He was promoted to the rank of Major-General November 29, 1862 History does not reveal the name of a braver, more fearless soldier. He was no spy-glass general, safely lodged on the hill-tops far away, but in the thickest of the fight his commanding figure could always be seen among the boys in blue, giving words of encouragement and command. The record of his personal daring at the battle of Williamsburg is a golden page in the annals of fame. Hancock had obtained a position of vantage; it was on a crest within twelve hundred yards of Fort Magruder. The Confederates sought to dislodge the bold intruder with an overwhelming number of men. They came with a rush, yelling "Bull Run! Bull Run! That flag is ours!" Hancock knew that the supreme moment had arrived. Leaving his place behind the line, and when the enemy were but forty yards from his brave boys, bareheaded, and mounted on his splendid charger, he dashed along the blazing front, between two solid walls of musketry and cannon, hailing a perfect storm of bullets and balls, he shouted, "Forward! Forward! For God's sake, forward!" The men, recognizing their fearless commander, with a great shout, charged upon the rebels, drove them back and gained the day. Another deed of unparalleled heroism was at the battle of Gettysburg, on Seminary Ridge. History does not record the like of this terrific fight; it was a veritable artillery duel. The air was hot with shot and shell, and bullets fell as thick as rain drops. The infantry hugged the ground, the gunners were being blown to pieces; to escape death was only a possibility. At this awful moment, amidst the hiss and rush of thousands of flying missiles, "Hancock, the Superb," mounted at the head of his staff, with the corps flag unfurled, rode along the "terrible crest" from the right of his line to the extreme left, furnished a rare example of sublime courage, and, with a bravery born of the hour, again perched victory upon the stars and stripes. No wonder the American people called him "Hancock, the Superb."

His civic career was no less brilliant than his military. While in command of the fifth district in 1867 at New Orleans, he conscientiously endeavored to enforce, equitably and justly, the laws in the States of Louisiana and Texas. In 1880 he was nominated for President by the Democratic party. At the time of his death, which occurred on February 9, 1886, he was stationed on Governor's Island, near New York City.

Hancock was a modest soldier, and dearly loved by all his men. When the wires brought the news of the demise of this great commander many a boy that wore the blue brushed something off his cheek. He needs no marble shaft to rear its lofty head to heaven to tell posterity his fame. No brass statue with blazing torch to light the vista of ages. His deeds, his noble deeds, valor, sublime character will live forever in the hearts of his countrymen. When the end of time is announced, and the recording angel draws aside the curtains of heaven, on the great scroll will be written in letters of living light, among the grandest characters of all times, the name of "Hancock, the Superb."

"THE ANCHOR AND SHIELD."

Response by W. W. Dodge, at a banquet of the Ancient Order of United Workmen, at Burlington, Iowa, July 20, 1886.

The national games of Greece were called the Olympic, founded, according to mythological history, by Jupiter himself. They were celebrated in Olympia, in Elis, and continued for five days in midsummer. Vast numbers of spectators came from far and near to visit the exciting sports. Not only did the exercises consist of exhibitions of bodily strength, such as running, leaping, wrestling, throwing the quoit, and hurling the javelin, or boxing, but also contests in music, poetry, and eloquence. It would appear these interesting exciting games and customs of the ancients are handed down to the modern, and by him fully and heartily enjoyed. Flattered by a kind invitation from your Order I have been an humble aider and abettor to the days of enjoyment. My services were most willingly and cheerfully given. Understand me, however, I do not claim to possess the desire or prowess to enter the contest in music, poetry and eloquence, but submit the strife for these garlands to others far more capable than myself.

I am a stranger to your order, but, permitted by your courtesy, I speak as a man to men. A thought begotten of your beautiful badge suggests a theme for some brief remarks. Emblazoned on it are sun-rays, an anchor, the shield. Sun-ray denoting charity· the anchor, hope; the shield, protection. Fit subjects for the poet's pen or the artist's brush. Would that my lips were touched by the "attic bee," that I might possess the power to dwell, with words eloquent, upon a subject radiant with beautiful conceptions. There is charity, greater than the other two graces, faith and hope. What a world of gladness is in the word. To the homeless wanderer it is healing sent on wings of sleep, or dew to the unconscious flower. To the hovel of the poor it is golden sunshine, blessed light of happier days. It may serve as the cross to which the unhappy maiden clings for salvation, and anchors her hope for pardon and futurity. To the man of vice it is the Bethlehem star, whose blessed light may lead him unto eternal joy. Workmen, let the "sun-rays of charity" ever guide your pathway, and each act done in its holy name will inure to your everlasting credit in the great book. The present day sees the ablest and the richest men kneeling in the temple of Mammon, with solemn faces and iron grasp holding urns filled with gold and precious jewels—rich offerings to their God. The pathetic wail of Hiawatha for his poor Minnehaha in the cabin of famine never reaches their sordid hearts. They wilfully shun that lovely mantle which "covereth a multitude of sins."

Hope! What is life without hope? An aimless existence; a ship without a rudder; an island without a people; a book without a plot; a diamond without lustre; youth without happiness. We must hope for the morrow. Live with hope. Hope to be good, to be charitable, to be loved and esteemed, and to be written on the great scroll, by an angel's hand, as Abou Ben Adam, "one who loves his fellow man."

There is the "shield," emblematic of protection. What is life, liberty and happiness without the protecting arm of the law? We venerate the constitution and the flag of our country, shields to the liberties we now enjoy.

Love of virtue protects the innocent; honesty stays the

tempter's hand; the wing of the eagle covers the little ones. Your fraternal ties environ wife and child with an armor stronger than the mail of the valiant knights of old. Workman, ever keep burnished the armor of your manhood and character; let the "sun-rays" of charity be felt wherever you are; the anchor of hope dropped in the clear water of truth; your shield a protection to widow and orphan.

Ancient Order of United Workmen, let me congratulate you on the selection of a badge that so fitly typifies your good and noble work, and may success and prosperity ever be the lot of your association.

"KNIGHTS OF THE FOOT BOARD."

Response by W. W. Dodge, at a banquet given at the National Convention of the Brotherhood of Locomotive Engineers, in the City of Burlington, Iowa, July 19, 1886.

Mr. President, Members of the Brotherhood of Locomotive Engineers, Ladies and Gentlemen:

This is the second time in my life I have been honored with an invitation to address brotherhoods of railroad men. Last year I spoke to a splendid body, the Brotherhood of Brakemen. Now it is permitted me to speak to the bronzed and stalwart knights of the locomotive. I can assure you that I highly appreciate this privilege. I am free to admit that I must be given "sand" when "pulling out" my remarks in the presence of these brave, expert men. It is therefore with fear and trembling that I open "my throttle;" and if I do not "burst a flue," I hope to make a reasonable progress and get there on "card time." I also appreciate the fact that Grand Chief Arthur is the "headlight" of this occasion, and has the "right of way." I am "running wild," and must needs be careful, lest I "jump the track" and have a bad "smash up." So I crave your indulgence and patience during my desultory remarks, and should you discover that my "drivers are slipping on the grade," call for the "air-brakes."

You have designated this day for a union meeting of

your Brotherhood, the place selected the oldest and best city in Iowa. Burlington, like wine, improves with age. Our city shows every evidence of modern advancement; nine railroads, a magnificent system of water works, this Grand Opera House, new stores, residences, and other attractions too numerous to mention. Our popular mayor has hung the latchstring on the outer walls; our worthy and hospitable men extend to you a brotherly hand of welcome; while our beautiful young ladies, God bless them, will meet you with bright faces wreathed in winning smiles, and make you for the moment wish that you were not married, that you might take one home with you. As for you single men, all I have to say is that we have numerous ministers and Justices of the Peace.

There are others here to-day better acquainted with the subject than I, who may relate the wonderful growth of railroads in this and other regions. They may relate the thrilling experience of Stephenson's engine, "The Rocket," which fifty years ago, with a load of thirteen tons, including many passengers, traveled at the rate of fifteen miles an hour, and the engine of Braithwait & Erickson, of London, moved at the astonishing speed of twenty-eight miles an hour. "It seemed, indeed," said a spectator, "to fly; presenting one of the most sublime spectacles of human ingenuity and human daring the world ever beheld. It actually made men giddy to look at it, and filled thousands with lively fear for the safety of the individuals who were on it, and who seemed not to run along the earth, but to fly, as it were, on the wings of the wind."

It sounds like one of Gulliver's phantasms when we are told that in 1830 in the United States there were only twenty-three miles of track in operation. Now we have an extent of 125,000 miles, costing, with equipments, about seven billion dollars, and affording employment to about 500,000 persons. The railroads of the world give a grand aggregate of 264,826 miles, of which we have about one-half in this country.

It was recently said by a United States Senator that "among the servants of our civilization none have approached the efficiency of the railway. It has annihilated distances; it has not only made the wilderness blossom like the rose, but it has enabled the rose to be readily exchanged for the products of the cities. It has conduced to the widest diffusion of labor, and rendered nations measurably homogeneous."

I learn that twenty-three years ago your Brotherhood was founded at Detroit, Michigan. Your first division was known as "The Brethren of the Footboard," and consisted of twelve members. You have now some 20,000 members in your Brotherhood, contained in 320 divisions. Your association is among the oldest labor organizations, and stands to-day as firm as any. The corner-stones of your grand Order are "Sobriety, Truth, Justice, and Morality." Your Brotherhood is eternal, standing on such a sublime and magnificent foundation. These principles are as lasting as the rock-ribbed hills. Engrave them on your hearts. Be true to them and you will stand before your fellow men as one of the "noblest works of God."

The life of a locomotive engineer is filled with sunshine and shadow. There is pleasure, there is sorrow on each side of the line. The merciless dagger of grief pierces the heart, while again the golden rays of joy make glad. Who has not observed the pride and affection lavished by a "Knight of the Footboard" on his engine? It is only equalled by the admiration and love of Pygmalion for his statue of ivory. Pygmalion was a sculptor, and with his skilled hand made a statue of ivory more beautiful than any living woman; it looked like the workmanship of nature. He fell in love with his own creation, and caressed it, and like unto a girl, he made it presents of flowers, birds, bright shells and beads of amber. At the festival of Venus, before the altar where sacrifices were offered, Pygmalion timidly said, "Ye gods, who can do all things, give me, I pray you, for my wife"—he dared not say, "my ivory virgin,"—but said instead, "one like my ivory virgin." Venus heard his prayer, and causing the flame on the altar to shoot up thrice into a fiery point, gave life to the subject of his creation.

So with the man of the lever on the nation's birthday festival. I have seen him bedeck his engine with flowers, pictures, gay colored ribbons and beautiful wreaths, until, like a bride, ready for the altar, it seemed to me he almost felt inspired to utter the prayer of Pygmalion.

In this rambling talk I could not hope to fitly portray the noble character of the locomotive engineer. His dauntless courage, fidelity to duty, willingness to sacrifice even life to save those in his charge, his seeming disregard of all danger, and heroic deeds, are themes for the poet and historian, rather than orator. His name is engraven on tablets of brass in the temples of everlasting fame. His virtues, valor, fidelity, sacrifice, shall shine as brilliantly and long as the lamps in heaven. Therefore, let us bear in mind that

"The sweetest lives are those to duty wed,
    Whose deeds, both great and small,
    Are close-knit strands of one unbroken thread,
    Where love ennobles all;
The world may sound no trumpet, ring no bells,
    The book of life the shining secret tells."

"THE UNCERTAINTY OF THE LAW."

"The law is a sort of hocus pocus science that smiles in your face while it picks your pocket, and the glorious uncertainty of it is of mair use to the profession than the justice of it."—Macklin.

Response by Hon. John B. Green, of New York City, at the second annual banquet of the Commercial Law League of America, at Omaha, July 21, 1896.

Mr. President:—It is a cardinal canon of post prandial oratory that the speaker should say nothing about the sentiment assigned him as a topic. And the etiquette of polite society forbids one on social occasions to talk shop.

To us who spend our days

"Mastering the lawless science of our law,
That codeless myriad of precedent,
That wilderness of single instances,
Thro' which a few, by wit or fortune led,
May beat a pathway out to wealth and fame."
—Tennyson.

such canons seem worthy of superstitious observance.

But this sentiment is as tempting as New England Johnny cake, or as old-fashioned molasses candy, and I am reluctant to make my remarks too much like Josh Billings' celebrated lecture on milk, which, though containing not even an allusion to lacteal fluid, was nevertheless literally on milk, because the lecturer continually sipped milk from a glass brought for the purpose.

The author of this sentiment was an Irish actor named McLaughlin, who preferred to be called Macklin, and who lived to the age of 107 years, but with so little title to fame that he is not accorded the honor of a biographical notice in the standard authority of the United Kingdom. But as authors are like death in loving a shining mark, he has much company in railing at the profession.

. Since the days recorded in the Scriptures indicating the origin of judges going on circuit: "And he went from year to year in circuit to Bethel, and Gilgal and Mizpah, and judged Israel in all those places"—1 Samuel, vii., 16, lawyers have been a favorite target for the biting shafts of literary wit.

The attorney is a gentleman by Act of Parliament, and he has been defined, with more wit than verity, as a learned man who rescues your estate from your enemy and keeps it for himself.

It was Ben Jonson who spoke of lawyers:

> "That could speak
> To every cause and things mere contraries,
> Till they were hoarse again."

And Butler wrote:

> "Is not the winding up of witnesses,
> And nicking, more than half the business?
> For witnesses, like watches, go
> Just as they're set, too fast or slow."

And Gay said:

> "I know you lawyers can, with ease,
> Twist words and meanings as you please,
> That language by your skill made pliant,
> Will bend to favor every client;
> That 'tis the fee directs the sense,
> To make out either side's pretense."

Goldsmith, too, has his fling: "Laws grind the poor and the rich men rule the law," was the curt observation in the "Traveller."

But it is not difficult to strike back.

It is Charles Reade who, in "Foul Play," permits his hero to be convicted of forgery and sentenced to penal servitude, without an effort to postpone the trial, notwithstanding the absence of a witness lying delirious with fever, by whom his innocence could be established, and who had been actually subpœnæd. While the celebrated trial of Shylock vs. Antonio, before the Venetian Common Pleas (see 3 Shakespeare's reports, 247), probably contains more reversible errors than any other reported case. And the result was the grossest injustice. In that trial the court held the condition of the bond valid, in the face of declaring it a design against life, which made it void as against public policy. But having held the condition enforcible, the court declared that in the case at bar the law did require a vain thing, a single exactly sufficient cut without shedding blood, and granted the main relief while denying its necessary and inevitable incidents. The plaintiff, finding the court would enforce the penal part of the bond only under conditions impossible of performance, claimed his legal right to judgment for the return of his loan with interest, when he is met with the astounding ruling that by refusing a previous tender, not only was any collateral he had released and the running of interest stopped, but any recovery of the principal was forever barred. And he is driven out, wronged of his just dues, and without indictment or trial heavily fined for an attempt at murder evidenced alone by a document the court had already held a lawful instrument.

We have to own that there are times, however, when just complaint is made of the glorious uncertainty of the law. This is due to two causes: (1) The stupidity of the judges; and (2) the omniscient wisdom of jurymen. When the young lawyer was interrupted in his citation of authorities to sustain elementary principles, by the remark from the bench that the court might be presumed to know some law, he very properly retorted that he had rested on that presumption in the court below and lost his case, and he did not mean to be caught that way again.

Many of us, I am sure, have at times felt like that learned

counselor, who, on being threatened with a commitment for contempt of court, blandly said that he had expressed no contempt for the court, but had on the contrary carefully endeavored to conceal his feelings.

And in all the lawyer's litany there is no more fervent prayer than "From jurymen who know it all, Libera nos, O! Domine."

When I hear complaints of the law's delay, I think with reverence of the observation of Sir Thomas Clarke, Master of the Rolls: "There are two things against which a judge ought to guard—precipitancy and procrastination." Sir Nicholas Bacon was made to say, which I hope never again to hear, that a speedy injustice is as good as justice which is slow.

There are different kinds of uncertainties, and some puzzling cases are held to be glorious to others than professors.

"What was the most confusing case you ever had?" asked a doctor of a lawyer. "Case o' champagne," returned the lawyer. "I hadn't got half through it before I was all muddled up."

This is the kind of litigation we have been participating in at Omaha.

When this banquet shall be deserted, and the remnants of this festal board have grown cold; when the waiters shall linger mournfully over these empty bottles and sadly collect the scattered corks, may your slumbers be as peaceful and your dreams as iridescent as the memories your guests will carry home. We return to tell our friends of tawny days when life among you was like swimming with silver fins and ivory gills in purple seas, of nights filled with music, and of mounting with gilt-edged pinions to meet the star-led dawn. And as we tell the story of our visit to those who missed it, the gurgling of Dead Sea cocktails will be as the sound of many waters. For, in the future, when we look into the kaleidoscope of memory, we will note no brighter bits of color than those which the shadows of our visit cast upon the glass. Nor shall a fairer spectre thread the crystal chambers of the brain than she whose jeweled forehead bears the name of Omaha.

"THE LADIES."

"O, woman; lovely woman! nature made thee
To tempt man; and we had been but brutes without you.
Angels are painted fair to look like you;
There is in you all that we believe of heaven,
Amazing brightness, purity and truth,
Eternal joy and everlasting love."
—Thomas Otway (Venice Preserved, Act 1, Sec. 7).

Response to above sentiment. at Omaha Convention of the Commercial Law League of America, by Martin Saxe, of New York City, July 21st, 1896.

Toastmaster, Ladies and Gentlemen:—It is very unfortunate for you that I notice by the clock that the hour is close at two, because the gentleman who follows me has asked me to help him out, and positively declines to speak before three o'clock. I, therefore, must ask your indulgence for the arduous work before me.

It is also unfortunate that I am not an after-dinner speaker. In order to try and fill the requirements of this toast, I wanted to read "Bird on Toast," but Judge Green, of New York, who has just made such an elaborate speech, got hold of the book this afternoon and would not give me a chance to use it. The chairman was quite clever in not caring to read the sentiment of this toast, and I am going to follow his example, as it is much too difficult to recite. Mr. Gray, this handsome gentleman from Chicago, on my left, tells me that he was responsible for the quotation.

You may all join me in singing "Gray's Elegy" to-morrow.

But first of all I want to say a word about the hospitality of the people of Omaha. Now, in my experience, I have enjoyed a great many visits to places far from home, but really none appealed so much to my sense of enjoyment as this one.

The first night I reached the town I was rushed off to the Coliseum, and after having my handsome carcass riddled with holes till you could see daylight through it, I was turned into a "Knight of Ak-sar-ben." Now, that was hospitality for you, and I was a fit subject for the hospital.

But I am here to speak about the ladies. I want to speak particularly about the ladies of Omaha. You all know that New York is noted for its handsome men; you can judge of the truth of that fact by the members of the New York delegation here to-night. Omaha is noted for its beautiful women. But what I admire more than the beauty of the women of Omaha is their patriotism. Really, in these times, it does one an immense amount of good to see the evidence of true patriotism in American women. The other night, when I was hugely enjoying myself at the dance at the Creighton Theater, surrounded by a bevy of your most charming belles, I was "right in it," so to speak, until Uncle Sam's officers came from the fort, and then I was deserted. Was not that patriotism for you? Really, the women of Omaha are truly patriotic; they are living pictures of the American flag!

> Their arms white as the bars,
> Their cheeks rosy as the stripes,
> Their eyes brighter than the stars,
> Women of God's fairest types.

But now I ought to say something about ladies in general, and I am going to try to show you what a wonderful effect women have had on the developments of the law. Probably this is not apparent at first blush, but I feel sure you will be convinced of it after what I am going to tell you. I know of one instance where a lady desired to have drawn a power of attorney. When the instrument was finished and handed to her to read, she noticed that it began, "Know all men by these presents." She at once raised an objection to this phrase, and desired the word "women" to be added. Her suave attorney replied politely, "Why, don't you know that man embraces women?"

I also recollect where a young widow came into the office of a brother attorney. She was crying profusely.

"My dear madam," said the lawyer, "there is no need of your carrying on so. You will get your third out of the estate."

"You are very bold, sir," she replied. "I have only just buried my second."

But, to come back to the ladies of Omaha, I want to tell you that one thing I noticed particularly was the great happiness, which is so very apparent, of the young married couples. It is a delightful thing to see, and in contrast to it I am reminded of a very sad story, which really should not be told on such a bright occasion as this, but I want to use it as a sort of a moral, and would ask you, therefore, to refrain from indulging in tears as far as possible.

The story is one of two Germans who were steadfast friends and both in love with the same young lady. Their names were respectively August and Herman. The object of their individual affection possessed the beautiful name of Matilda. In the course of time Herman succeeded in winning the affections of the young lady, and married her. Notwithstanding his success, the friendship, which had at no time time been injured by the rivalry, remained as before.

A year or so after the marriage, Herman was suddenly called to Germany. Before going he went to August and said: "Mine frient, I must go avay. You are mine vife's best frient—I leafe her in your care; you vill look out for her;" then sailed away.

On his return August met him at the gang-plank of the vessel. His face was pale, and his eyes red and swollen. As he clasped Herman's hand he could hardly speak. He said, "Herman, prepare yourself for de vorst."

"Vat is der matter?" Herman asked anxiously.

Someting terrible! Matilda is tead!"

Herman stopped a moment. "Don'd make me laf; mine lips are chapped."

But I must not go on in this way any longer. I am here to toast the ladies. Now then—

Here's to the ladies of Omaha,
Whose beauty's noted far and wide;
The best of wives, the best of mothers,
God bless them all! God bless the others.

(The toastmaster said he would not in this instance read the sentiment under the toast, as there was but one audience before which he could do it justice, and that that audience was an audience of one—his wife.)

"THE UNITED STATES OF AMERICA."

Response by John L. Webster, delivered at the Omaha banquet of the Commercial Law League of America, July 21st, 1896.

Mr. Chairman, Ladies and Gentlemen:—When Washington had delivered his farewell address as the first President of the United States, he was given a banquet at Philadelphia, at which was exhibited in his honor an allegorical painting. The central figure in that painting was a woman representing America, seated on an elevation composed of sixteen marble steps, representing the several states of the new nationality. On her left was a shield, the sign of protection, and an eagle, the bird of freedom. At her feet lay the cornucopia, overflowing with the blessings to mankind secured by the American revolution. In her right hand she held the Indian calumet of peace, supporting the cap of liberty. In the perspective appeared the temple of fame, in which the memory of Washington should be forever sheltered. On her left hand was an altar dedicated to public gratitude, indicative of that gratitude which now swells in the hearts of more than sixty-five millions of people In her left hand she held a scroll inscribed "Valedictory"—that document so full of wisdom and statesmanlike advice that it has ever since served as an anchor of public safety At the foot of the altar lay a plumed helmet and sword, emblems of the many victories of the revolutionary fathers, but now laid aside as the Goddess of Liberty ruled above them in peace.

The figure of Washington appeared retiring down the marble steps, pointing with his right hand to the emblems of power he had resigned, and over his head Genius was placing a wreath of laurel.

That allegorical painting was a beautiful picture of the newly risen republic, which had its birth amidst the storms of seven years of war, and had but lately started on its more brilliant career of peace.

That is the nation which has gone on developing for more than one hundred years, extending her territory, increasing and expanding her industries and spreading her commerce, until she has become the mistress of the world, and the home and the refuge of the oppressed people of all other nations who have sought her shelter and her protection.

It is a nation which has an object to serve and a destiny to meet. I might say of her as Seward once said: "I would have you consider what a nation it is of which you are governors—a nation quick and vigorous of thought, free and bold in speech, prompt and resolute in action, and just and generous in purpose—a nation existing for something, and designed for something. * * * Why else was this nation chosen, that out of her as out of Sinai should be proclaimed and sounded forth the tidings and trumpet of political reformation to all nations."

We believe with Washington that the mission of our

country is one of peace and not of bloodshed. It was during a reign of peace that our nation acquired the territory included in the Louisiana purchase, the territory included in the Florida purchase, thus widening and extending our territories until the nation clasped in its embrace all the land between the Atlantic and the Pacific.

It was during a reign of peace that our nation established the principles of the Monroe doctrine; that the United States would not brook with indifference the interference of any European power with the domestic concerns of any nation upon the American continent; neither would we submit to any further enlargement of European possessions upon the American continent.

With the expansion of territory came power, and with power the fulfillment of the mission of this country, that the western continent should be the home of republics and the land of freedom.

To the accomplishment of universal freedom it was necessary for the most enlarged freedom within our own territory. Slavery must give way to liberty. That liberty did not have its birth in the embraces of peace, but out of the hot convulsions of war.

War may be terrible and destructive; it annihilates and destroys; it eats flesh and it drinks blood; but out of such havoc and disaster may come blessings.

Out of the war of the rebellion there was created the greatest and most lasting benefits. The people are happier and the nation is stronger. The quietude and slow progress of the old times have given way to the rapid progression and solidifying strength of the new. Before we were a simple union of States. Now we are a banded union, whose supremacy is recognized by the old world.

War is not in all things evil, although almost universally condemned by men of peace, and theorists. War is frequently as beneficial as it is sublime. It was war which created the freedom of the States after the declaration of '76;

it was war which perfected the union of the States after '61.

I might almost apply to the war of the rebellion the words which Victor Hugo wrote of the wars of the French revolution:

"The French revolution is the greatest step in advance taken by mankind since the advent of Christ; incomplete it may be, but it is sublime. It loosened all the sacred bonds of society; it softened all hearts, it calmed, it appeased, enlightened; it made the waves of civilization to flow over the earth; it was good. The French revolution is the consecration of humanity."

Prior to 1860 it did seem that America had reached the acme of perfection, and was rapidly traveling along the highway to the fulfillment of her destiny. But it was not so. Another event greater than all those that had gone before was left for the administration of Abraham Lincoln, the apostle of liberty.

Lincoln surveyed the whole history of the past, from Washington to Jefferson—from Jefferson to Monroe—from Monroe to Buchanan. He looked into the future and saw the realization of his prediction, "A house divided against itself cannot stand." That house must be reunited, no matter how severe the struggle, how great the cost, how terrible the hardship, how extensive the bloodshed. He foresaw the trials and tribulations which would beset his path, and he gave utterance to his feelings when he was about to take his departure from his fellow-citizens in Springfield, to take upon himself the labors of President of the United States, when he said, "I go to perform a task more difficult than that which devolved upon Washington."

The task was to save the union of States from dissolution and shipwreck, amidst the storms of sectional passion then blowing a furious gale, that had its beginning over the slavery question, and which was to divide the national household unless it should become permanently free. It was but a few years before that Daniel Webster had said:

"Freedom, human liberty and human rights are gaining the ascendant on earth." They were gaining the ascendant on earth, but they had not reached it. While we were proclaiming forth the tidings and trumpets of political reformation to other nations we had not secured that liberty to all our own people. That liberty which had been given them by God, but which had been wrested from them by man. For a time it seemed that this republic was to be bound like another Prometheus to the adamantine rock, while slavery like another vulture was preying in its vitals.

The disguised blessing of war furnished the opportunity for the issuing of the greatest of all documents in the cause of freedom, human liberty and human rights spoken of by Webster—the emancipation proclamation—a document as sacred to the American people as the American constitution, and which put an end to the buying and selling of the image of God like a beast in the market. It came as the result of war, and it could not have come without it. Thus by war was liberty born. Thus by war was the household reunited. Thus by war was the nation saved. Thus by war was it made greater and nobler than ever before, purified as by fire, sanctified by patriot blood, and glorified as of God.

For this act historians have written of him as the benefactor of mankind. Orators have praised him in the warmest and most eloquent words of panegyric. Sculptors have chiseled his form in marble; while slaves with broken shackles were kneeling at his feet. Artists have painted him on canvas with that emancipation scroll in his hand. But Lincoln as I view him was greater than all that. His aim was broader and more comprehensive. He loved the union of the states. He saw the destiny of the nation expanding through the mists of the future, destined to become an example of what Republican form of government might do and ought to do to ameliorate the condition of mankind, of all races and all creeds, and that the government he was to save was to dominate the western hemisphere.

The liberating of the slaves, grand though it be in thought as well as in action, was but the means to an end. Lincoln's purpose was to save the union which Washington had created, and Jefferson enlarged, and Monroe protected. To save the Union under the Constitution, with slavery if he could, but without it if he must. His love for the Union was greater than all other loves, and stood out superior to all other considerations. How beautifully he pictured that thought in the closing sentence of his inaugural address:

"The mystic chords of memory, stretching from every battlefield and every patriot grave, to every living heart and hearthstone all over this broad land, will yet swell the chorus of the Union, when again touched, as they surely will be by the better angels of our nature."

The nobleness of his nature and the purity of his patriotic purposes will never be expressed in words more chaste and touching than these, in which he pictured the love of his country.

Oh, that we had a sculptor with the genius of Canova who could picture him in his true greatness. I know not what that monument would be—but in some form it would represent a patriotic saint, likened somewhat to the Bartholdi statue of liberty enlightening the world.

Oh, for the genius of that Raphael who painted the transfiguration; of that Titian who painted the assumption of the Virgin Mary—to put on canvas that Lincoln we knew and the world knows. I know not what such a painting would be, but in some form it would be his apotheosis with the millions who love our country watching his enrollment among the saints.

Lincoln left us that nation of which Seward spoke, "Existing for something, and destined for something; having for her destiny the working out of political reformation to all nations." She is the mistress of her own future. By the teachings of her example she is setting in motion the creation of republican forms of government all over the western hemisphere. By her prowess and her greatness she may change the systems of Europe. Now firmly established on the broad foundations of liberty, she has risen to a prodigious power. She has conquered more by peace for the cause of humanity in one hundred years than did Rome by arms in many centuries. She has become the wonder of the world, and yet her duty has but begun. Her march must still be forward, by the ways of peace if possible, but if wars must needs cross the pathway which she must tread to the accomplishment of that purpose for which she was chosen as out of Sinai, let the war come, and her patriotic sons will meet it manfully.

With her freedom has come justice, and with justice has come patriotism, and with patriotism assured strength and length of days. She has stayed the rushing waves of iron rule in her sister states of South America. She has become the breakwater against European spoliation and conquest on this side of the ocean. She is destined to rule the American continent north and south, for this continent is her domain. North America has become the home of the Anglo-American race. In time we shall all belong to one family, which shall have the same civilization, the same language, the same religion, the same habits, the same manners, and from which thought will circulate in the same form and betray itself in the same colors. These results, with our memories of Washington, and Jefferson and Monroe, and Lincoln, shall become bonds of union so strong that neither wars of conquest nor wars of ambition can break them asunder. Already she has reached the realization of the vision of John Bright: "I see one vast confederation stretching from the frozen north in unbroken lines to the glowing south, and from the stormy billows of the Atlantic westward to the calmer waters of the Pacific; I see one people and one law and one language and one faith, and all over that wide continent the home of freedom and a refuge for the oppressed of every race and every clime."

"There is a land of every land the pride;
Beloved of heav'n o'er all the world beside.
*　　*　　*　　*　　*　　*
Where shall that land, that spot of earth be found?
Art thou a man?　A patriot?　Look around.
Oh, thou shalt find, howe'er thy footsteps roam
That land thy country, and that spot thy home."

"THE LAWYER OF THE SOUTH; What He Has Been, Is Now and Expects to Be."

Response by Hon. Hill Montague, of Richmond, Va., at the first annual banquet of the Commercial Law League of America, at Detroit, August 15, 1895.

Mr. Toastmaster, Ladies and Gentlemen: When I was requested the other day to respond to this toast, I did not know that I would be called upon to act upon that much-abused committee, known as the Committee on Permanent Organization of this Convention, and our duties have been so arduous that I have not had time to write my remarks, and I have almost lost my voice this afternoon in trying to prevent our getting apart too much. And while so many have already gone, yet the beating of my heart on this occasion would not allow me to keep my seat when asked to respond to this sentiment. It is a big subject, "The Lawyer of the South: What He Has Been, Is Now, and Expects to Be." It was in the early dawn of this century that the Southern lawyer became known as one of the strong arms of our Government. It was at the close of the last century, a little more than a hundred years ago, that a Southern lawyer in old St. John's Church, Richmond, stood up and said in that tempestuous crowd, "Give me liberty or give me death." I am afraid some of you will echo that sentiment here before long. It was a Southern lawyer who penned the Bill of Rights, that wonderful instrument that guarantees to us freedom of conscience, of speech and of the press. It was a Southern lawyer who penned that remarkable document, the Declaration of Independence.   It would take too long to run along this list, but we might mention the names of Patrick Henry, of Madison, of Monroe, and of Sargent Prentice, men who have honored the Southern land, but no less honored our whole united Union. And what shall I say of the lawyers of to-day? In order to tell you of the lawyers of to-day I must needs take you back in your thoughts a little more than thirty years ago, when the strong tide of war burst over the Southland, and for four long years this country knew a civil strife unequaled in the annals of history.   But the Southern lawyer went out into our battlefields, many of them spilt their life's blood there in defense of what they believed to be right, but on that memorable day at Appomattox they yielded up the sword to the valorous Grant, the man who received it with so much magnanimity from our honored Lee. (Applause.) After they had silently stacked their arms they took down their musty books and started again the practice of law.   And to-day we have men there who are honoring their profession.   Men who, while they have the warm blood of the South, yet are more progressive, more industrious, and more in keeping with the forward march of the times. We might mention to you the men to to-day, among them William L. Wilson, John W. Daniel, Speaker Crisp, Senator Morgan, and others equally great.   But we must pass on.   Among the distinguished law writers of the South of the present day, and of the days that are passed and gone, your minds will recall those of Judah P. Benjamin, the man who has given us the foremost work on jurisprudence; and then John D. Miner, of my own State, who has furnished us with his "Institutes"; and J. W. Daniel, whose "Negotiable Instruments" are accepted as authority in every State in this Union.   And now let me say—I have only spoken seven minutes; I always close on time—let me say that this is not the time nor the place to make long speeches at this late hour, but it has done my heart good to come here from the South and to tell you that out of the ashes of the Old South there has arisen a New South and loyal to the new Union, and to-day we can shake hands and march on to victory and to success, and woe be to the outsider who comes against us. (Applause.) Let me say, Mr. Toastmaster and ladies and gentlemen, in bidding you adieu, that I trust from the bottom of my heart that each lawyer here present may so practise his profession through honesty, integrity and industry as to be able to chisel out of the rough-hewn rocks of life a valuable and successful career. (Applause.)

"THE LADIES: May Their Virtues, Like Their Sleeves, Never Grow Less."

Response by Hon. Ernest T. Florance, of New Orleans, at the first annual banquet of the Commercial Law League of America, at Detroiit, August 15, 1895.

Mr. Toastmaster, beautiful columns, empty chairs and tables, and all that is left—left of the six hundred—I am going to get an audience if I have to count them all in. I echo the sentiment of Patrick Henry, for if we do not soon give you liberty I am afraid we will give you death. I was puzzled when I heard the applause with which my rising was greeted. I thought at first it was due to the fact the sentiment was the ladies, and then I remembered it was the last toast of the evening. I have not understood why a person of my sex was asked to respond to this toast. It is many and many a year since I was a lady, and judging from the little I know of them, they are generally accustomed to answer for themselves, and judging from those that we have had with us to-day, who came up and voted like little men— and some of them voted twice on the same question—I think they could have taken charge of the sentiment in their own favor. But who can think of woman without remembering those beautiful lines of the poet:

Oh, woman, in our hours of ease,
Uncertain, coy and hard to please,
But grown at last familiar with her face,
We first endure, then pity and then embrace.

(Laughter.) My friend, Mr. Montague, tells me I have mixed up two quotations, but when it comes to the question of women, I am very likely to mix up everything. From the land of the magnolia to the land of the pine, from the great gulf of the Southland to the great lakes of the Northland, from the length and breadth of this land, I carry to woman this message from our profession: In the words of Ruth to Naomi, Where thou goest will we go, and where thou dwellest there will we dwell; thy people (particularly thy mother-in-law) will be our people, and thy will our will; and when thou diest we shall die, and where thou art buried we will be buried, and, for my own part, as soon as that happens, I am ready to get buried. (Applause and laughter.) One of our friends has told you a beautiful tale. I will tell you another. When the alphabet was first made there was a great controversy among the letters as to which one was to form the most important word. The first letter of it said, "I am the first, and should form the most important." "No," said the middle letter, "I am the center of all things, and I should have that right." "No," said the last, "I am the end of all things, and that must be the most important thing for man." And so the great inventor of language, in order to harmonize that strife, created the word truth out of the first, the middle and the last letter of the alphabet. And whenever I hear that story I am reminded of woman, not particularly on account of her connection with truth, but because she is the beginning and the center and the end of all things that concern man. I suppose you will ask what has this to do with woman? I don't know. I don't know anything about women, and I never saw a man who did know anything about them. (Laughter and applause.) She to me has always been a terra cotta—**Mr.**

Montague again nudges me and says I mean terra incognita. Well, if "she" refers to the new woman—she is a terror anyhow, and the more you attempt to explore her the less you will find out about her. I believe thoroughly in the words of Mr. Nye, "There ain't no telling what a woman is going to do until she has done it, and then it ain't no use." A clever man once told me that an after-dinner speech should consist of a jest, an anecdote and a sentiment. I have reversed them two or three times in my remarks, and with your permission, Mr. Chairman, I will end with an anecdote. At the end of the last war one of the colored soldiers, who fit nobly, returned to his old master. The master said: "Pompey, you were in the war, were you not?" "Oh, yes, I was in de wah." "Did you fight?" "Oh, yes, I was darh." "And did you do your duty, Pompey?" "Oh, yes, yes; I obeyed orders." "Ah, now, give me an instance." "Well, boss, in one of the battles, when the shot was coming mighty thick, the captain he said to us boys, 'Strike for your country and your homes.' Most of the other fellows struck for de country, but I struck for my home." Now, I advise you all at this late hour, my friends, to strike for your homes.

❧Speeches and❧
❧Speech Making❧

By Judge J. W. Donovan.

No book of interest to lawyers, law students, or young men generally, published within recent years, has obtained a more immediate and wide-spread popularity than Judge Donovan's "Speeches and Speech Making." It seems to have made an instant hit. This is doubtless because it is a practical book, and gives ideas, suggestions and helps both as to preparing and delivering speeches. Judge Donovan has sought in writing this book to give young men who are ambitious to become speakers something that will be of practical help to them in attaining that end. In addition to the ideas and suggestions as to the preparation and delivery of speeches, it contains examples of speeches for different occasions, and altogether contains many helps for one wishing to become a successful speaker. Men who are frequently called upon to make speeches, and what lawyer, young or old, is not, will find this book valuable. A man who intends or expects to make many speeches cannot begin his preparation too early, for when called upon he has no time to prepare, and must depend upon the preparation of times past. This book will aid one to prepare for such occasions. The sooner a man begins to prepare, the better, for he cannot become a good public speaker at a bound. Public speakers are made as well as born.

Handsomely Bound in Cloth, $1.50, Delivered.

...Address the...

Sprague Publishing Co.,
DETROIT, MICHIGAN.

The Comic Blackstone

By Gilbert A'Beckett.

THIS is a book that was written more for the entertainment than the instruction of lawyers and law students, and the author, being a true humorist, has made it very interesting. It is amazing to note how many opportunities for fun he has found in the Commentaries. It may be as dry as "the dry bones of the law" to one who has never studied law, but to the lawyer and law student it is one of the most interesting and amusing books ever written. To the lawyer or law student, however, it will be found to be more than merely amusing. It is also a practical aid or supplement to the study of Blackstone. It is remarkable how thoroughly a point of law may be impressed on one's mind by a joke, and A'Beckett's Comic Blackstone is full of instances of this kind. It contains many hearty laughs and much good law, and no lawyer or law student who has a touch of humor in him can fail to appreciate it highly.

Price, handsomely bound in cloth, $1.25.

THE SPRAGUE PUBLISHING CO.,

Booksellers and Publishers,

DETROIT, MICH.

Choosing a Specialty.

THIS is the title of a book-let containing eleven articles, treating of eleven different specialties in the practice of law, and the various considerations that a man should weigh in determining upon any particular line of practice as his specialty, such as education and special qualifications required, peculiarities of the practice, if any, nature of the work, the class of clients to be dealt with, compensation to be expected, etc. These articles were written by eminent men in their particular line of practice, and first appeared in The Law Student's Helper, where they attracted much attention throughout the country, and were widely quoted. The articles and their authors are as follows:

Criminal Law, by John G. Hawley, one of the authors of Hawley & McGregor on Criminal Law, Detroit, Mich.

Mining Law, by John B. Clayberg, Helena, Montana.

Patent Law, by Albert H. Walker, author of Walker on Patents, Hartford, Ct.

Medical Jurisprudence, by Marshall D. Ewell, M. D., LL. D., Dean Kent College of Law, Chicago.

Real Estate Law, by Darius H. Pingrey, author of Pingrey on Real Property, Bloomington, Ill.

Commercial Law, by Hon. Daniel K. Tenny, Madison, Wis., late of Tenny, McConnell & Coffeen, Chicago.

Law Teaching, by Prof. Edwin H. Woodruff, of the Cornell Law School, Ithaca, N. Y.

Insurance Law, by D. Ostrander, of Chicago.

Admiralty Law, by Martin Clark, of Clinton & Clark, Buffalo, N. Y.

Corporation Law, by Charles F. Mathewson, of Strong, Harmon & Mathewson, of New York.

General Practice, by John B. Green, of Cole & Green, of New York.

This list of papers from writers of such standing and ability, cannot fail to contain much of interest to every lawyer and law student.

Price, 50c, delivered.

THE SPRAGUE PUBLISHING CO., DETROIT, MICH

Eloquence and Repartee in the American Congress...

By Wm. C. SPRAGUE.

A book in which the editor has collected many of the most interesting and notable events of a particularly notable Congress. viz: the Forty-Second Congress. This Congress sat during the famous Reconstruction Period, and the ability of its members, together with the importance of the questions then agitating the country, united to produce many exciting scenes, many great debates, many flights of eloquence, and many flashes of wit and repartee between the members, among whom were some of the greatest men whose names illumine our history. To the student of American history, and to the student of eloquence, this book will have an absorbing interest. Illustrated with numerous half-tone portraits.

Handsomely bound in Cloth, $1.50.

THE SPRAGUE PUBLISHING CO.,

Publishers and Booksellers, DETROIT, MICH.

Flashes of Wit from Bench and Bar...

By Wm. C. Sprague.

"Much given to speech and seasoned anecdote,
And wit and repartee of Bench and Bar."
—*Valentine.*

THIS is one of the brightest books that has been issued in recent months. The nature of its contents is amply indicated by its title. Every page literally flashes and scintillates with the ready wit of some leader of the bar or some brilliant occupant of the bench. Every one of its two hundred pages contains many hearty laughs for the reader. Such a fund of anecdote and story will not be found within the covers of any other book now on the market. It contains some of the purest, brightest and happiest examples of wit and humor ever collected by an appreciative editor. One who often speaks in public will find these stories mirth-provoking, and every one knows the value of a taking story properly interjected into a public speech, or in conversation.

Handsomely bound in Cloth.

PRICE, $1.50 DELIVERED.

Address **THE SPRAGUE PUBLISHING CO., Detroit, Mich.**

Study Law at Home

The Sprague Correspondence School of Law, of Detroit, Michigan, prepares you right in your own home for examination for admission to the bar. It selects the proper text books; it maps out the proper course; it helps you over the rough places; it shows you how to learn everything worth learning, and how to avoid the non-essential matter; it gives you thorough examinations, and fits you in every way for active practice. For those who do not feel prepared to take up a regular course in law, it furnishes a Preparatory Course

of three months, which every man and woman, and every boy and girl whether proposing to practise law or not, should study. It also furnishes a Business Law Course, the most thorough course on Business Law that can be had anywhere. Whether or not you desire to practice law, you should enroll yourself as a student in this School, and use your spare moments in useful study along practical lines. The law forms an exceedingly interesting study, and is a splendid course for general culture. A handsome catalogue with testimonials from practising attorneys, free. Remember that our system only requires that you devote to it your spare moments.

Address The Sprague Correspondence School of Law,

M ajestic Building, DETROIT, MICH.

Office Portraits.

Justices of the Supreme Court of the United States.

Group picture giving all the Justices who ever sat on the Supreme Bench of the United States, with the date of their birth, death and appointment, and the State from which appointed, making a pictorial history of the court. A fine artotype, making a picture 19x24 inches, printed on heavy paper, with wide margins. This picture is the work of the celebrated artist Bierstadt, and is printed in steel plate ink. Very handsome. $7.00 delivered.

One Hundred and Forty-four Eminent American, English and Canadian Lawyers.

Two fine engravings, 28x38 inches, with each portrait 2¼x3¼ inches. With these engravings go a two-volume work with the Life Sketches, Thoughts, etc., of the lawyers whose portraits are given in the engravings. Regular price, $15.00. Our price $10.50 delivered.

The Present Supreme Court of the United States.

This is a photograph, 14¼x20¼ inches, mounted on boards 20x24 inches. Gives the United States Supreme Court as now constituted. Price, $3.00.

Blackstone.

Steel engraving by John Sartain. 12x15 inches, printed on heavy paper, with wide margins. This is a very fine portrait, but we are able to furnish it while our supply lasts, for $3.00 delivered.

Joseph H. Choate.

Photogravure, 8x6¼ inches, printed on heavy paper, with wide margins. $1.00.

Frederick R. Coudert.

Companion piece to the Choate portrait. $1.00.

The Present Justices of the United States Supreme Court.

Half-tones, each 5x3¼ inches, on good paper, with ample margins. 50 cents each.

Chief Justice Marshall.

Full length portrait, 16¼x10¼ inches. Very handsome. Price, $2.00.

Chancellor James Kent.

Fine steel engraving, 15x10 inches, printed on fine heavy paper, 23x30 inches. Very handsome office portrait. Price, $5.00, delivered.

THE SPRAGUE PUBLISHING COMPANY,

Detroit, Michigan.

Quiz!══Quiz!══Quiz!

D O YOU KNOW of any better method of impressing upon your mind what you have read than questions and answers? We do not, and this method has been endorsed by all thinkers since Socrates. And how much more valuable it is when questions have been selected by a master, so that they cover just the points that you should remember, and bring out all the phases of each subject, many of which you would never notice in merely studying the text-book, and show its many sides and in different lights in a way that is most beneficial to the student, but which is foreign to the nature of text-books. But a properly conducted Quiz should not be a mere aid to the memory. It should not be confined to showing the student how much or how little he knows. It should be instructive in the highest sense. Naturally, the answering of the questions compels the student to both remember and think, but the questions should also be so framed as to teach him to think, as by suggesting new phases of the subject and new lines of thought, and by calling for reasons and principles as well as mere rules. The questioner should never be satisfied with a mere parrot-like repetition of the text-book, and the questions should be so framed that that will not be sufficient.

With these principles in mind we have had prepared a series of quiz books which we call the Quizzer Series. That they are helpful to the students, we have the highest evidence, viz.: large sales and students who have bought one book, coming back for subsequent numbers. Each book consists of two parts, Part I containing the questions and being interleaved with blank pages on which the student may write his answers, and Part II containing the correct answers and explanations.

Here is the list. Some new ones are just out. You can't do the best work without them.

Have you them all? Fill out your set QUICK.

Blackstone Quizzer A (on Book 1 of Blackstone),	-	50 cts.
" " B " 2 "	- -	50 cts.
" " C " 3 "	-	50 cts.
" " `D " 4 "	- -	50 cts.
Kent Quizzer E (on book 1 of Kent's Commentaries), -	-	50 cts.
" " F " 2 " "	-	50 cts.
" " G " 3 " "	-	50 cts.
" " H " 4 " "	-	50 cts.
Quizzer No. 1. Domestic Relations,	- -	50 cts.
" No. 2. Criminal Law,	- -	50 cts.
" No. 3. Torts,	- -	50 cts.
" No. 4. Real Property,	-	50 cts.
" No. 5. Constitutional Law,	-	50 cts.
" No. 6. Contracts, -	-	50 cts.
" No. 8. Common Law Reading,	-	50 cts.
" No. 9. Corporations, -	-	50 cts.
" No. 10. Bills, Notes and Checks,	-	50 cts.
" No. 11. Equity, -	- -	50 cts.
" No. 12. Agency,	-	50 cts.
" No. 13. Partnership, -	-	50 sts.
" No. 14. Sales of Personal Property,	-	50 cts.
" No. 15. Evidence,	- -	50 cts.

☞ OTHERS TO FOLLOW.

Address, THE SPRAGUE PUB. CO., Detroit, Mich.

Valuable Monographs

Hawley's Law of Arrest.—Price, 75c.

This is a little book of 70 pages by John G. Hawley, the distinguished legal writer, stating the principles of the law of arrest, including the rights and duties of police officers in and before making arrests, the rights and duties of private citizens in making arrests, the rights of individuals in the matter of being arrested, the liabilities of officers and citizens for false imprisonment, warrants—their form and when necessary and when not necessary to the legality of the arrest, rights of prisoners, etc. Thousands of copies have been sold to the Police Departments throughout the country, to lawyers and law students and to the general public.

Hawley's Law for Tenants—Price, 75c. A book of 78 pages bound in leather, explaining clearly the mutual rights and obligations of landlord and tenant in such plain, simple language that every person interested may understand the law on the subject and guard himself against entering into an improvident contract. It is published with a view of furnishing a safe guide to the layman as well as a good reference book to the lawyer and the law student.

Hawley's Law for Land Buyers—Price, 75c. This little book contains 56 pages, and treats fully of the law of Real Property as met with in every day transactions in real estate, it having to do with the contract, the title, the deed, the mortgage, fixtures, right of possession, warranties, homestead, record, etc. Every dealer in the land should be possessed of this little treatise. Bound in leather.

Shall I Study Law?—Price, 50c. By one who has tried. Paper bound, 69 pages. The book is written for young men who are thinking of taking up the law as a special study, and giving reasons for and against it, together with much practical instruction, enabling young men to know what to do in answer to this question.

Our National Charters—Price, 50c. This book contains the Declaration of Independence, the Articles of Confederation, the Constitution and Amendments, Washington's Farewell Address, the Dictatorship Conferred on Washington, the Ordinance of 1787, the Monroe Doctrine, and the Emancipation Proclamation.

Requirements for Admission to the Bar—Price, 50c. Giving the rules and regulations of all the States and Territories.

How to Prepare for a Civil Service Examination—Price, 50c. Paper, 100 pages.

How to Build Up a Successful Commercial Law Practice—Price, 50c. Paper, very practical. By A. X. Dunner.

The Vest Pocket Parliamentary Pointer—Price, 25c. This little book answers at a glance the intricate questions of Parliamentary Law, without diagrams or reference marks to confuse or mislead. It is so small it can be concealed in the hand, and referred to during a meeting without attracting attention. It contains about 22 pages, and measures about $2\frac{1}{2}$x4 inches. It uses a system of abbreviations, condensing parliamentary rules into the smallest space.

The British Constitution—By Amos Dean, LL. D. The British constitution is one of the greatest monuments of worldly wisdom that the centuries have to bequeath to us. It is the work of thirty generations of statesmen. No student of political philosophy should omit to study it. This makes an excellent text book. Cloth 50c, delivered.

The Sprague Publishing Co.,

Publishers and Booksellers, DETROIT, MICH.